10-MINUTE CARDS
TO GIVE & SHARE

EDITED BY TANYA FOX

HOUSE of
WHITE
BIRCHES

PUBLISHERS
SINCE 1947

10-Minute Cards to Give & Share™

EDITOR	Tanya Fox
ART DIRECTOR	Brad Snow
PUBLISHING SERVICES MANAGER	Brenda Gallmeyer
ASSOCIATE EDITOR	Sue Reeves
ASSISTANT ART DIRECTOR	Nick Pierce
COPY SUPERVISOR	Michelle Beck
COPY EDITORS	Nicki Lehman, Mary O'Donnell
	Beverly Richardson
TECHNICAL EDITOR	Läna Schurb
PHOTOGRAPHY	Justin P. Wiard
PHOTO STYLIST	Sherry Johnston
GRAPHIC ARTS SUPERVISOR	Ronda Bechinski
GRAPHIC ARTISTS	Erin Augsburger, Pam Gregory
PRODUCTION ASSISTANTS	Cheryl Kempf, Marj Morgan,
	Judy Neuenschwander
PUBLISHING DIRECTOR	David J. McKee
BOOK MARKETING DIRECTOR	Dwight Seward
EDITORIAL DIRECTOR	Gary Richardson

Printed in China
First Printing: 2006
Library of Congress Control Number: 2005938349
Hardcover ISBN-10: 1-59217-121-4
Hardcover ISBN-13: 978-1-59217-121-7
Softcover ISBN-10: 1-59217-122-2
Softcover ISBN-13: 978-1-59217-122-4

FROM THE EDITOR

At one time or another, all of us have needed a last-minute card for a special occasion. For card-making enthusiasts, buying one just isn't an option.

Not having a lot of time to create a card doesn't mean you have to forfeit great design or style. Quick and easy doesn't mean plain and simple, and you'll see just what I mean when you create one of the fabulous cards included in this collection … in just 10 minutes!

Choose from more than 140 creative designs featuring various techniques and tools to help you get started. Rubber-stamped and rub-on images or sentiments are a quick way to add a little or a lot of color to your creation. A subtle dusting of glitter is a sure method for jazzing up a quick card. Premade shaker bubbles add a fast bit of fun movement, and photographs are the ideal way to create truly unique and personalized greetings. Embellishment possibilities are endless—a shimmery ribbon, a few rhinestone brads or intricate corner punches turn ordinary cards into little works of art!

The end result is sure to be a hit, and no one will ever suspect that it just may have been a spur-of-the-moment creation!

Happy crafting,

CONTENTS

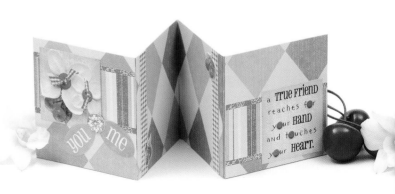

DIE CUTS
78

Die cuts are available in a myriad of shapes and sizes—or make your own with a die-cutting machine and your choice of printed papers.

DIMENSIONAL EMBELLISHMENTS
94

With this technique, anything goes! Add a bit of this or a touch of that to quickly personalize a handmade greeting.

RUB-ONS & STICKERS
116

Rub-on transfers and stickers are often the bearers of sentiments for your cards, but they can also deliver artwork, from whimsical to photo-realistic.

STAMPING
134

Grab a rubber stamp and an ink pad and go wild! Create designs as simple or as intricate as time allows.

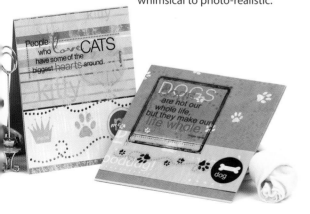

HIGH-TECH & PHOTO CARDS

Even if you don't have a digital camera, you can still use these high-tech ideas on your cards. Most photo-processing labs can transform your treasured photographs into digital images and save them on a CD. Your picture-editing software does the rest!

You're How Old?

DESIGN BY KATHLEEN PANEITZ

Cut 1⅝ x 5½-inch strip of printed paper with stripes on left half and dots on right half; adhere to left side of card front as shown.

Trim photo to 3⅝ x 3⅜ inches; adhere in upper right corner of card, ¼ inch from edges.

Apply rub-on transfer in lower right corner of card. Tie ribbon in a bow; trim ends at an angle. Center and adhere bow at bottom edge of photo. ■

SOURCES: Card from Die Cuts With A View; printed paper from Heidi Grace Designs Inc.; ribbon from May Arts; rub-on transfer from Making Memories; glue from Beacon.

MATERIALS

4¼ x 5½-inch white card

Pastel stripes/dots printed paper

Birthday candles photo image

"YOU'RE HOW OLD?" rub-on transfer

⅜-inch-wide pink-stitches-on-black grosgrain ribbon

Paper glue

Snow Scene

DESIGN BY TAMI MAYBERRY

MATERIALS

Light blue card stock

Light blue snowflake
printed paper

Transparency sheet

Black-and-white snow scene
photo image

Small plastic snowflake
embellishments

Iridescent glitter flakes

⅛-inch-wide white satin
ribbon

Envelope template to fit 6½
x 5-inch card

1-inch-wide border stickers

Craft knife

Double-sided tape

Adhesive foam tape

Glue

Form a 6½ x 5-inch card from light blue card stock. Trim snow scene photo image to 6 x 4½ inches; center and adhere to front of card.

Using a craft knife, cut a 5½ x 4-inch opening in center of a 6½ x 5-inch piece of light blue card stock, forming a frame. Adhere a 6½ x 5-inch piece of transparency to back of frame with double-sided tape.

Adhere strips of foam tape around edges of photo; make sure there are no gaps in the tape. Pour glitter flakes and snowflake embellishments into box formed by tape. Adhere card-stock frame with window over foam tape, pressing edges firmly.

Cut two 6½-inch strips and two 5-inch strips of ribbon. Adhere ribbon strips along outer edges of photo frame on front of card, 1/16 inch from edges, crisscrossing ribbon ends at corners.

Use envelope template to create an envelope from snowflake printed paper. ∎

SOURCES: Printed paper from American Traditional Designs; glitter flakes from Magic Scraps; snowflake embellishments from Sarah Heidt Photo Craft; envelope template from Green Sneakers Inc.

Vintage Christmas

DESIGN BY STACEY STAMITOLES

Form a 5-inch-square top-fold card from red card stock. Adhere a 4⅞-inch square of printed paper to front of card.

Print vintage photo or Christmas clip art onto printable canvas paper; trim to 4⅞ inches wide. **Option:** *Use copy of vintage photo or vintage-style image from magazine or book.* Mat photo onto red card stock; adhere to front of card.

Referring to photo for placement, adhere ribbon and card-stock embellishment across bottom of card using adhesive dots. Thread "happy holidays" charm and a short length of ribbon onto safety pin; adhere with adhesive dots. ∎

SOURCES: Printed paper and card-stock embellishment from Design Originals; safety pin and charm from Making Memories; adhesive dots from Therm O Web.

MATERIALS

Red card stock

Brown/white printed paper

Inkjet-printable canvas

Digital image of vintage photo *or* Christmas clip art on computer; *or* copy of vintage photo; *or* Christmas image from magazine or book

Christmas-themed card-stock embellishment

¾-inch green safety pin

Silver "happy holidays" charm

⁷⁄₁₆-inch-wide red-and-green ribbon

Paper glue

Adhesive dots

Tea Time

DESIGN BY KATHLEEN PANEITZ

MATERIALS

5½ x 4¼-inch white card

White card stock

Printed papers: lavender
  polka dots, apricot
  handwriting

Teacup photo image

Rub-on transfers: flower,
  "THINKING of YOU"

Paper glue

Adhere a 3¼ x 4¼-inch piece of lavender printed paper to left side of card front. Adhere a 2¼ x 4¼-inch piece of apricot printed paper to right side of card front.

Trim photo to 3¼ x 2⁷⁄₁₆ inches; adhere to 3½ x 3-inch white card stock as shown.

Apply "THINKING of YOU" rub-on transfer to white margin below photo. Apply flower rub-on transfer to lower right corner of card stock, overlapping photo.

Adhere photo panel to front of card. ■

SOURCES: Card from Die Cuts With A View; printed papers from Scenic Route Paper Co. and Making Memories; rub-on transfers from K&Company; glue from Beacon.

Dreams

DESIGN BY TAMI MAYBERRY

Form a 4 x 6-inch card from black card stock. Adhere a 3¾ x 5¾-inch piece of striped printed paper to front of card.

Draw "stitched" outline along edges of a 3-inch square of green card stock with black fine-tip marker. Referring to photo for placement, adhere to front of card.

Use computer and photo-editing software to convert flower image to black-and-white and crop it to 3 inches square. Using white font, add "Dreams" across center of flower. Print photo; trim and adhere to front of card on top of green square. **Option:** *Use a flower photo print; add "Dreams" with white gel pen or alphabet rub-on transfers.*

Use computer to generate, or hand-print, "Dreams are the flowers that bloom in your heart" in black ink on green card stock; trim to 3¼ x 1⅞ inches. Adhere to bottom of card.

Use envelope template to create an envelope from striped printed paper. ∎

SOURCES: Printed paper from Sweetwater; envelope template from Provo Craft.

MATERIALS

Card stock: black textured, green textured

Light green/black/white striped printed paper

Photo paper

Digital flower image *or* photo print

White gel pen *or* white alphabet rub-on transfers (optional)

Black fine-tip marker

Envelope template to fit 4 x 6-inch card

Double-sided tape *or* glue stick

Computer with photo-editing software and printer

Vintage Cupid

DESIGN BY STACEY STAMITOLES

MATERIALS

Printed paper: pink, green

Vintage cupid image

Black distress ink

Silver oval "Love" charm

Metallic round decorative brad

2 pink mini brads

1⅝-inch pink paper flower

Pink fibers

Paper piercer *or* large needle

Paper glue

Form a 5-inch-square top-fold card from green printed paper; ink edges. Adhere a 1½ x 4-inch piece of pink printed paper to front of card, referring to photo for placement.

Trim cupid image to 3 x 4½ inches; ink edges. Adhere to front of card as shown. Attach "love" charm using pink mini brads. Attach paper flower with decorative brad. Wrap fibers around fold of card; knot on outside, near right edge. ■

SOURCES: Printed papers from Basic Grey; distress ink from Ranger Industries; charm from All My Memories; decorative brad from Making Memories.

Easter Blossom

DESIGN BY SUSAN HUBER

Form a 4¼ x 5½-inch card from lavender card stock.

Adhere a 3¾ x 5-inch piece of pink card stock to a 4 x 5¼-inch piece of white card stock.

Referring to photo, attach silk flower petals to assembled panel with lavender mini brad. Adhere panel to card front.

Use computer and script font to generate "Easter" in purple ink to fit within an area measuring 3⅜ x ½ inch. Print onto transparency; trim to 4⅛ x ⅞-inch. **Option:** *Apply purple word or alphabet rub-on transfers to spell "Easter" onto a 4⅛ x ⅞-inch piece of transparency sheet.*

Attach transparency strip to card front with pink mini brads as shown. Stamp "Happy" near left edge just above transparency strip. ■

SOURCE: Rubber stamp from Making Memories.

MATERIALS

Card stock: lavender textured, pink textured, white

Ink-jet transparency sheet

Regular transparency sheet (optional)

"Happy" rubber stamp

Mauve dye ink pad

Easter sticker *or* rub-on transfer (optional)

Mini brads: 1 lavender, 2 pink

2 (1¾-inch) layers of silk flower petals

Paper piercer *or* large needle

Adhesive

Computer with color printer

MATERIALS

5½ x 4¼-inch light blue card

Card stock: yellow, light blue

Flower photo

2-inch "thank you" acrylic
    ribbon slide

⅞-inch-wide yellow-and-
    white gingham-checked
    ribbon

Fine-grit sandpaper

Adhesive

Sunny Day Thank-You

DESIGN BY SHERRY WRIGHT

Trim photo to 4 x 3½ inches; sand edges lightly. Adhere to 4⅜ x 3⅞-inch piece of yellow card stock. Adhere matted photo to front of card, referring to photo for placement.

Thread a 6½-inch piece of ribbon through acrylic slide. Position slide as shown; adhere to front of card. Adhere ribbon ends to reverse side of card front.

Adhere a 5¼ x 4-inch piece of light blue card stock to reverse side of card front, covering ribbon ends. ■

SOURCES: Card and card stock from Paper Salon Inc.; ribbon slide from Pebbles Inc.

Sunshine & Seashells

DESIGN BY SHERRY WRIGHT

Cut a line of diamonds from printed paper; adhere across card front.

Trim photo to 3½ x 3⅜ inches; sand edges lightly. Adhere photo to 4 x 3⅞-inch piece of turquoise card stock. Adhere matted photo to front of card ⅛ inch from top edge and ¼ inch from right-hand edge.

Adhere fabric embellishment near upper left corner of card as shown. ■

SOURCES: Card, card stock and printed paper from Paper Salon Inc.; fabric embellishment from me & my BIG ideas.

MATERIALS

5½ x 4¼-inch yellow card

Turquoise card stock

Yellow/turquoise/white harlequin printed paper

Seagull photo

"Sunshine and seashells" fabric embellishment

Fine-grit sandpaper

Adhesive

Freedom

DESIGN BY SUSAN HUBER

MATERIALS

Textured card stock: red, blue

3 patriotic-themed 1⁵⁄₁₆ x 1¾-inch card-stock stickers

1-inch foam alphabet stamps

White acrylic paint

4 assorted red, white and blue ribbons and rickrack

Navy blue mini brad

1-inch silver star spangle

Mini buttons: red, white, blue

Paper piercer *or* large needle

Adhesive

Form a 5½ x 4¼-inch top-fold card from red card stock. Adhere a 5½ x 1-inch strip of navy blue card stock to front of card ⅝ inch from top.

Adhere stickers across blue strip using foam tape, spacing evenly. Adhere 5½-inch pieces of rickrack and ribbon below stickers.

Stamp "Freedom" in lower left corner of card using white paint. Attach star spangle to lower right corner of card with mini brad. Adhere mini buttons randomly over "Freedom." ■

SOURCES: Stickers from Pebbles Inc.; foam stamps from Li'l Davis Designs; ribbons and rickrack from Fibers By The Yard; star spangle from Making Memories.

My Dear Friend

DESIGN BY LINDA BEESON

Form a 5½ x 4¼-inch card from white card stock.

Trim downloadable printed or purchased printed paper to 4¾ x 3½ inches. Adhere to 4⅞ x 3⅝-inch piece of turquoise card stock; adhere this piece to a 5⅛ x 3⅞-inch piece of light green card stock, then adhere double-matted printed paper to front of card.

Apply "My dear friend" rub-on transfer to printed paper toward lower right corner. ■

SOURCES: Digital scrapbooking kit from 2 Peas in a Bucket; rub-on transfer from The C-Thru Ruler Co.

MATERIALS

Textured card stock: white, light green, turquoise

Printed paper: downloaded from an Internet source *or* a digital scrapbooking kit *or* purchased

Satin-finish photo paper (optional)

"My dear friend" rub-on transfer

Double-sided tape

Computer and printer (optional)

Autumn

MATERIALS

Card stock: light green
    textured, pumpkin
Leaves printed paper
Ink-jet transparency sheet
    (optional)
1¼-inch round metal-
    rimmed tag
Leaf rubber stamp
Dark orange ink pad
4mm green ombré ribbon
Deep gold fiber
1-inch circle punch
Adhesive
Adhesive foam tape
Computer with printer
    (optional)

DESIGN BY SUSAN HUBER

Form a 5½ x 4¼-inch card from light green card stock.

Randomly stamp a 5¼ x 1½-inch strip of pumpkin card stock with leaf images. Cut a 5¼ x 2½-inch piece of leaves printed paper. Referring to photo, adhere card stock and paper to card front. Adhere a 5½-inch piece of ribbon over seam.

Thread dark gold fiber through hole in tag. Punch a 1-inch circle from printed paper and adhere to tag. Adhere tag to card with adhesive foam tape.

Apply rub-on transfers to a 5 x 2-inch piece of transparency sheet or use a computer to generate the word "Autumn" and print onto transparency sheet.

Referring to photo, adhere transparency to card. ∎

SOURCES: Printed paper from Paper Fever; rubber stamp from A Muse Artstamps; fiber and ribbon from Fibers By The Yard.

Blessings

DESIGN BY LINDA BEESON

Form a 5½ x 4¼-inch card from light green card stock; ink edges with brown inkpad.

Alter photo on computer using photo-editing software: Blur photo edges and add sentiment, including a shadow, if desired, for higher contrast. Print photo onto satin-finish paper and trim to 4¾ x 3⅝ inches. **Option:** *Trim regular photo to size and add sentiment using rub-on transfers.*

Center and adhere photo to 4⅞ x 3¾-inch piece of brown card stock, then adhere to front of card. ■

MATERIALS

Card stock: light green textured, brown

Digital photo *or* printed photo

Satin-finish photo paper (optional)

Thanksgiving-themed rub-on transfers (optional)

Brown chalk ink pad

Double-sided tape

Computer with photo-editing software and printer

PUNCHES

These specialized tools cut graceful corners and photo mounts as well as openings for lace weaving, ribbon slits and holes for inserting brads. You can use the shape that was punched out, or the piece of paper from which it was punched—two design elements in one!

Snowflake Dreams

DESIGN BY SUSAN HUBER

Wrap sheer ribbon vertically around a 4 x 5¼-inch piece of snowballs printed card stock; knot on front near top. Trim ribbon ends at an angle; slide to right-hand half of card stock.

Attach large metal snowflake over ribbon with large white brad as shown. Adhere card-stock panel to front of card.

Open card; punch three 1-inch holes down left side, ¾ inch from edge. Ink edge of center hole with silver leafing pen.

Punch a 1-inch circle from snowflakes printed card stock, centering a snowflake in the circle; ink edges with silver leafing pen. Apply rub-on transfers to spell "Dream."

Close card. Adhere punched snowflake circle to inside of card with foam tape as shown. Adhere smaller metal snowflakes on inside of card inside top and bottom punched holes. ∎

SOURCES: Printed card stock from Basic Grey; silver leafing pen from Krylon; rub-on transfers from Making Memories; metal snowflakes from Making Memories and Queen & Co.

MATERIALS

4¼ x 5½-inch top-fold blue-gray card
Printed card stock: snowflakes, snowballs
Silver leafing pen
¼-inch black alphabet rub-on transfers
1⅞-inch-wide sheer white ribbon
⅜-inch white brad
Metal snowflakes: 1¹³⁄₁₆-inch, 2 (1-inch)
1-inch circle punch
Adhesive foam tape
Adhesive

Spring Fever

DESIGN BY LINDA BEESON

MATERIALS

Card stock in assorted
    textures: white, light
    green, blue, yellow,
    salmon pink
Alphabet rub-on transfers
4 light gray mini brads
⁹⁄₁₆-inch flower punch
Paper piercer *or* large
    needle
Glue

Form a 5½-inch-square card from white card stock with fold at top.

Cut one 5½ x 1-inch strip from each remaining color of card stock. Punch flowers randomly from colored strips, reserving one flower of each color. Adhere strips across front of card as shown.

Using a paper piercer or large needle, poke a hole through the center of each reserved flower; poke a row of four holes ⅝ inch apart in lower right corner of card. Attach flowers to card with mini brads.

Apply alphabet rub-on transfers to spell "Spring Fever" as shown. ■

SOURCES: Rub-on transfer from Making Memories; punch from Papershapers.

Enjoy

DESIGN BY WENDY SEBESTA

Cut from printed paper: 3 x 4-inch piece of paisley, 1½ x 4-inch piece of numbers print, 3 x 2½-inch piece of orange polka dot, and 1½ x 2½-inch piece of argyle. Referring to photo, adhere pieces to front of card, edges touching, with paisley and numbers print pieces at the bottom, leaving a ⅛-inch border around outer perimeter.

Cut 5 x ½-inch and 7 x ½-inch strips from striped paper; adhere to front of card over seams between printed paper blocks. Trim paper strips even with edges of card.

Cut a 2 x 4-inch tag from white card stock. Punch a flower from polished stone printed paper; adhere to tag ⅝ inch from top; adhere epoxy sticker to center of flower. Apply "enjoy" rub-on transfer near bottom of tag. Clip paper clip over top of tag; adhere tag to front of card as shown. ■

SOURCES: Printed papers from Making Memories, KI Memories and Murdock Country Creations; rub-on transfer from Making Memories; epoxy sticker from Provo Craft.

MATERIALS

4¾ x 6¾-inch white card

White card stock

Pink/orange/yellow printed
   papers: argyle, paisley,
   polka dots, stripes,
   numerals, polished stone

"Enjoy" rub-on transfer

Small round epoxy-coated
   flower sticker

Small pink paper clip

2-inch flower punch

Glue

Swinging Christmas

DESIGN BY JENNIFER MCGUIRE

MATERIALS

Card stock: red, light brown, gray

¾-inch alphabet rubber stamps

Watermark ink pad

Assorted ¼-inch-wide striped and gingham-checked ribbons

Silver mini brad

3 tiny crystal faceted cabochons

Black fine-tip marker

Punches: ½-inch circle, 2-inch circle, ⅛-inch hole

Glue

Cut a 4¼ x 5-inch piece of red card stock and a 4 x 4¾-inch piece of light brown card stock. Punch a ½-inch circle and a 2-inch circle from light brown card stock.

Center light brown rectangle on top of red rectangle; center and punch a small hole through both layers near top edge. Punch a matching hole through center of small light brown circle; insert silver mini brad through holes.

Spread glue over 2-inch circle; cover with strips of ribbon. Trim ribbons even with edges of circle. Adhere ribbon-covered circle to front of card 1½ inches from top.

Draw an ornament hanger extending from circle "ornament" and up around mini brad using a black fine-tip marker. Adhere a ½ x ⁷⁄₁₆-inch gray card-stock rectangle to top of ornament, overlapping edge slightly.

Tie a piece of ribbon in a bow; adhere to top of ornament. Adhere three cabochons near right edge of ornament in a horizontal row, slightly below center. Using alphabet stamps and watermark ink pad, stamp "merry" on card front below ornament. ■

SOURCES: Rubber stamps from Hero Arts; ink from Tsukineko Inc.; ribbons from May Arts.

Believe in Santa

DESIGN BY SUSAN HUBER

Form a 4¼ x 5½-inch card from red card stock. Cut a 5½-inch piece from card-stock border; sand edges and adhere to front of card with adhesive foam tape, ⅜ inch from fold.

Cut a 3 x 4⅛-inch rectangle from green printed paper and a 2¾ x 3⅞-inch rectangle from blocks printed paper; sand edges lightly. Adhere small rectangle to large one; adhere to upper right corner of card ⅛ inch from edges.

Punch a 1⅛-inch circle from vintage Santa image, centering Santa in circle. Punch a 1½-inch circle from green printed paper. Lightly sand edges; adhere Santa circle to green circle with foam tape. Punch a ⅛-inch hole through top edge of green circle; knot ribbon through hole. Adhere to lower right corner with adhesive foam tape. ■

SOURCES: Printed paper and card-stock border from The C-Thru Ruler Co./Deja Views; Santa image from Altered Pages.

MATERIALS

Red textured card stock
Christmas-themed printed
    paper: green, green/red/
    tan blocks
¾-inch-wide green
    Christmas-themed card-
    stock border
Vintage Santa image
¼-inch-wide red ombré
    ribbon
Punches: 1⅛-inch circle, 1½-
    inch circle, ⅛-inch hole
Fine-grit sandpaper
Adhesive
Adhesive foam tape

Happy Valentine's Day

DESIGN BY SHERRY WRIGHT

MATERIALS

5½ x 4¼-inch white card

Brown card stock

Pink/brown/blue printed
    papers: paisley, flowers

Brown ink pad

2⅜-inch "happy valentine's
    day" chipboard
    embellishment

1³⁄₁₆ x 1¾-inch primitive-
    style heart punch

Adhesive

Ink edges of a 5½ x 4¼-inch piece of paisley printed paper and adhere to card front.

Punch three hearts from flower printed paper and three from brown card stock. Ink edges of printed paper hearts.

Overlap and adhere hearts in a row across bottom of card, alternating printed paper and brown card stock. Adhere "happy valentine's day" embellishment to lower right corner of card as shown. ■

SOURCES: Printed paper from Paper Salon Inc.; chipboard embellishment from Li'l Davis Designs; heart punch from EK Success Ltd.

Love Defined

DESIGN BY AMY YINGLING, COURTESY OF STAMPIN' UP!

Form a 4¼ x 5½-inch card from olive green card stock.

Stamp surface of 2 x 2⅛-inch piece of yellow card stock with definition stamp and yellow ink. Stamp natural ivory card stock with definition stamp and olive green ink; trim a portion of the love definition in a 1¾ x ¼-inch strip.

Punch a 1¼-inch circle from olive green card stock and a 1⅛-inch daisy from light blue card stock. Center daisy on circle; poke four holes in a square through center of daisy and circle. Thread linen thread though holes and make a cross-stitch; knot thread on back and trim. Adhere circle and daisy to yellow card-stock rectangle as shown. Adhere ivory card-stock strip with love definition across yellow card stock and olive green circle, tucking strip under daisy petals.

Adhere yellow panel to 3⅛ x 5½-inch light blue card-stock rectangle, ¾ inch from bottom.

Pierce an evenly spaced row of holes around yellow card stock with paper piercer. Adhere light blue card stock to front of card 1³⁄₁₆ inch from fold. ■

SOURCE: Card stock, stamp and ink pads from Stampin' Up!

MATERIALS

Card stock: light blue,
    natural ivory, olive green,
    yellow
"Love" definition
    background rubber stamp
Ink pads: olive green, yellow
Punches: 1¼-inch circle,
    1⅛-inch daisy
Linen thread
Large needle
Paper piercer
Glue

MATERIALS

Tone-on-tone printed
  papers: yellow stripes,
  yellow dots, orange dots,
  purple stripes, purple
  dots, blue dots, green dots
"Wish big" rubber stamp
Clear embossing powder
Black ink pad
Black fine-tip marker
2 flexible plastic pop-up
  blocks
Punches: corner rounder,
  ⅝-inch flower, 1-inch
  circle, 1½-inch circle,
  1¾-inch circle, 2-inch
  circle
Heat gun
Adhesive foam squares
Paper glue

Wish Big

DESIGN BY LINDA BEESON

Form a 4⅞ x 4½-inch card from yellow striped paper with stripes running vertically. Round bottom corners using corner rounder punch.

Card front: Cut a 1½ x 2⅝-inch rectangle for candle from purple dotted paper. Punch flower from yellow striped paper; punch 1½-inch circle from yellow dotted paper and 1¾-inch circle from orange dotted paper. Add outlining details to purple rectangle, punched flower and yellow circle using black fine-tip marker.

For candle flame, adhere flower to yellow circle, and yellow circle to orange circle; adhere completed flame to top of candle. Adhere candle to front of card ¼ inch from bottom using adhesive foam squares.

Card interior: For candles, cut a 1 x 2½-inch rectangle from blue dotted paper, a 1 x 2¼-inch rectangle from green dotted paper and a 1 x 3-inch rectangle from purple striped paper with stripes running horizontally. Punch three flowers and one 1¾-inch circle from yellow striped paper; three 1-inch circles from yellow dotted paper; and one 2-inch circle from orange dotted paper. Add details and assemble candles as above.

Referring to photo, adhere candles to each other. Adhere candles at fold of card using plastic pop-up blocks.

Adhere the 1¾-inch yellow circle to the orange circle. Stamp "wish big" on yellow circle using black ink; sprinkle with clear embossing powder and emboss. Adhere embossed circle inside card. ■

SOURCES: Printed papers from Making Memories; rubber stamp from Paper Salon Inc.; plastic pop-up blocks from JudiKins; flower and circle punches from Papershapers.

MATERIALS

Light blue textured card
    stock

Blue/green/lavender printed
    paper

"Celebrate" definition
    rub-on transfer

12 silver star brads

1½-inch-wide light blue
    grosgrain ribbon

Ink pads: blue, green, purple

Punches: 1¼-inch circle,
    corner rounder, ⅛-inch
    hole punch

Pinking shears

Instant-dry paper glue

Celebrate

DESIGN BY MARY AYRES

Form an 8 x 5-inch card from card stock. Round corners using corner rounder punch. Ink edges with blue, green and purple inks.

Cut a 4-inch piece of ribbon using pinking shears. Ink edges with blue, green and purple inks. Apply "celebrate" rub-on to ribbon; center and adhere to bottom of card.

Punch 12 (1¼-inch) circles from printed paper. Arrange circles on front of card in three vertical rows of four and adhere to card. Punch a ⅛-inch hole in the center of each circle and attach star brads. ■

SOURCES: Printed paper from KI Memories; rub-on transfer from Royal & Langnickel; glue from Beacon.

cel•ebrate (sel' e brat') *vt.*
1. to perform 2. to commemorate
(an anniversary, holiday or birthday)
with festivity 3. to honor publicly—
to have a good time

Floral Fantasy

DESIGN BY KATHLEEN PANEITZ

Adhere a 4¼ x 5½-inch piece of green printed paper to inside of card.

Punch three ¾-inch square openings down right side of card front, spacing them ½ inch apart and ⁵⁄₁₆ inch from right edge, and positioning the first opening ⅞ inch from top of card.

Adhere a 4¼ x 1-inch strip of yellow printed paper across card front as shown. Adhere a ⅝ x 4¼-inch strip of pink printed paper on front as shown.

Adhere the flower collage sticker to card front ⅜ inch from top and left-hand edges of card. Apply alphabet rub-on transfers to inside of card to spell "MOM" in square windows. ■

SOURCES: Card from K&Company; printed papers from Bo-Bunny Press; sticker from Penny Black Inc.; rub-on transfers from Heidi Grace Designs Inc.

MATERIALS

4¼ x 5½-inch ivory card

"Splatter" printed papers:
  green, pink, yellow

2½ x 4½-inch flower collage
  sticker

Alphabet rub-on transfers

¾-inch-square punch

Paper glue

MATERIALS

Card stock: gold, blue

Printed paper: blue/white/
gold/red diamonds, blue/
white/gold/red flowers

Friendship-themed rub-on
transfer

Small decorative round
stamp

Watermark ink pad

Gold square wire clip

Gold rickrack

Corner rounder punch

Adhesive

Sunshine of Life

DESIGN BY TAMI MAYBERRY

Form a 5 x 7-inch card from gold card stock. Adhere a 4¾ x 6¾-inch piece of diamond printed paper to front. Round all corners.

Round corners of a 4 x 6-inch piece of blue card stock. Stamp small round motifs randomly using watermark ink and adhere to front of card as shown.

Adhere a 4¼ x 3-inch piece of flowers printed paper to a 4¼ x 3¼-inch piece of gold card stock; adhere panel to front of card 1½ inches from top with right edges even.

Cut 3¾ x 1¾-inch pieces from blue card stock and gold card stock. Referring to photo for placement, adhere rectangles to front of card. Apply friendship-themed rub-on transfer to gold rectangle.

Adhere a 7-inch piece of rickrack vertically to front of card, ⅞ inch from fold. Attach wire clip over edge of flower printed paper and underlying gold card-stock rectangle. ■

SOURCES: Printed papers from Autumn Leaves; rub-on transfer from Royal & Langnickel; stamp from Close to My Heart; ink pad from Tsukineko Inc.; wire clip from Creative Impressions.

Just Peeking In

DESIGN BY TAMI MAYBERRY

Round corners of card. Punch heart from light pink card stock; adhere wiggly eyes to heart. Referring to photo for placement, adhere heart to upper left corner of card front.

Cut a 5½ x 4-inch piece of printed paper and round corners. Trim off upper left corner diagonally so the edge lies just below eyes; adhere to front of card.

Punch a balloon from pink card stock; trim end to form oval. Adhere below eyes with foam dot.

Adhere a 3⅛ x 1¾-inch brown card-stock rectangle to front of card. Use computer to generate, or hand-print, "Just Peeking In" in brown ink on light pink card stock; trim to 2⅞ x 1½ inches. Adhere to brown rectangle. ■

SOURCES: Printed paper from Chatterbox Inc.; balloon and heart punches from Uchida of America.

MATERIALS

5½ x 4-inch white card

Card stock: brown, light pink textured, pink textured

Brown/pink/white circles printed paper

Brown fine-tip marker (optional)

2 (½ x ⅝-inch) oval wiggly eyes

Punches: corner rounder, 1⅜-inch heart, ½-inch balloon

Adhesive

Adhesive foam dot

Computer with color printer

Thick & Thin

DESIGN BY LINDA BEESON

MATERIALS

Card stock: blue textured,
light green

Printed paper

2 card-stock multicolored
paint chip strips

"through THICK and THIN"
rub-on transfer

Punches: 1⅞-inch flower, ⁹⁄₁₆-
inch circle, corner rounder

Sewing machine with navy
blue thread

Fine-grit sandpaper

Paper glue

Form a 4¼ x 5½-inch card from blue card stock. Round corners of a 3⅞ x 5¼-inch piece of printed paper and adhere to front of card.

Trim one paint chip strip to 2⅝ x 4¾ inches and round corners. Sand edges lightly. Adhere to front of card as shown. Using zigzag stitch, machine-stitch through front of card along lower half of paint chip strip's left edge. Apply "through THICK and THIN" rub-on transfer as shown.

Punch flower from blue portion of second paint chip strip; punch ⁹⁄₁₆-inch circle from light green card stock for flower center. Adhere flower and center to lower right corner of card. ■

SOURCES: Printed paper from Basic Grey; rub-on transfer from Die Cuts With A View; punches from Papershapers.

It's All About You

DESIGN BY LINDA BEESON

Cut a 10½ x 6-inch piece of card stock with ribs running horizontally. Score card vertically 3½ inches from each side edge to form a three-panel card. Open card flat.

Fold left-hand panel over center panel and hold together; punch a 1¼-inch circle through both layers ½ inch from the lower right corner of the card front. Sandwich transparency over cutout circle between layers; glue closed.

Adhere a paper flower to transparency circles on front and inside of card. Center and adhere a crystal cabochon to center of each flower.

Apply rub-on transfers to front of card as shown. ■

SOURCES: Rub-on transfers from Making Memories; punch from Papershapers.

MATERIALS

Light green rib-textured
  card stock

1¾-inch square cut from
  transparency sheet

Word rub-on transfers

2 (⅞-inch) paper flowers

2 (¼-inch) clear round
  faceted crystal cabochons

1¼-inch circle punch

Glue

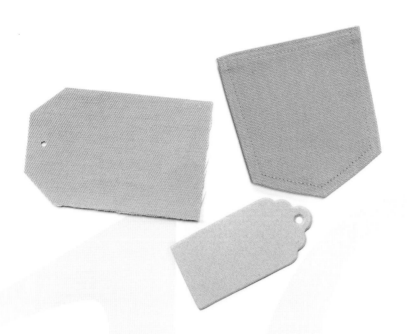

POCKET CARDS

Pocket cards hold all sorts of surprises within their pockets and pouches. Small treats, sticks of gum, gift certificates—how will you fill them?

Vintage Noel

DESIGN BY MARY AYRES

Form an 8 x 5-inch card from card stock.

Adhere photo-mounting corners to corners of a 7½ x 4½-inch piece of printed paper; adhere to front of card.

Apply rub-on letters to bottom flaps of envelopes to spell "noel." Attach stickers to tags and tie cord ties in a bow. Insert tags in envelopes.

Adhere envelopes with tags across front of card. ∎

SOURCES: Printed paper from K&Company; tags from Rusty Pickle; stickers from Crafty Secrets Publications; rub-on transfers from Making Memories; glue from Beacon.

MATERIALS

Cream card stock

Black text printed paper

4 (1⅝ x 2¾-inch) vellum
   envelopes

4 (1⅜ x 2¾-inch) distressed
   tags with cord ties

4 vintage Santa stickers

4 gold metallic photo-
   mounting corners

Alphabet rub-on transfers

Instant-dry paper glue

MATERIALS

Card stock: tan, light green

Printed paper

5¾ x 4⅜-inch light green
 envelope

1-inch-wide border stickers

Love- and happiness-themed
 rubber stamps

Red ink pad

1-inch-wide light green satin
 ribbon

Sewing machine with white
 thread

¼-inch-wide double-sided
 tape

Adhesive foam tape

My Love

DESIGN BY KAREN DESMET, COURTESY OF ANNA GRIFFIN INC.

Pocket: Cut a 4¼ x 5½-inch piece and a 4⅛ x 2-inch piece of light green card stock. Cut a 4⅛ x 5⅜-inch piece and a 4⅛ x 1⅞-inch piece of printed paper. Center and adhere large printed paper to large card stock and small printed paper to small card stock.

Lay smaller panel across larger one, bottom edges even. Using a narrow zigzag stitch, machine-stitch around edges of larger panel on all four sides, attaching smaller panel.

Center and adhere a piece of border sticker to a 4¼ x 1⅛-inch piece of light green card stock, then adhere strip across bottom of pocket.

Stamp love-themed sentiment on a 2¾ x ¾-inch piece of tan card stock. Ink edges, then adhere to border sticker with foam tape.

Tag: Adhere a 2⅞ x 4½-inch piece of printed paper to a 3 x 4⅝-inch piece of tan card stock. Using a narrow zigzag stitch, machine-stitch around edges.

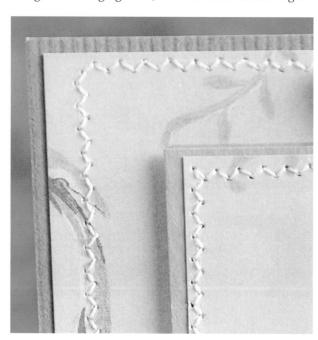

Stamp happiness-themed sentiment on a 2 x 1-inch piece of tan card stock. Ink edges and adhere to tag. Fold a 2½-inch piece of ribbon in half and adhere cut ends to back of tag. Tuck tag into pocket.

Envelope: Adhere a piece of border sticker across bottom edge of envelope. ■

SOURCES: Printed paper and border stickers from Anna Griffin Inc.; rubber stamps from Plaid/All Night Media for Anna Griffin Inc.; tape from Therm O Web.

Happiness IS

BEING WITH YOU

I love you dearly

Just for You

DESIGN BY ALICE GOLDEN

MATERIALS

5½-inch-square dark pink
    card

Patchwork printed paper

Embellished pink fabric
    pocket

2¾ x 1¾-inch white tag

Rubber stamps: "just for
    you," ⅞-inch flower

Pigment ink pads:
    sunflower, orchid

Lime chalk ink pad

¼-inch-wide blue-and-
    green gingham-checked
    ribbon

¼-inch-wide double-sided
    tape

Adhere a 5⁵⁄₁₆-inch square piece of printed paper to card.

Replace adhesive from back of fabric pocket with strips of double-sided tape applied down the sides and across bottom. Adhere pocket to card.

Randomly stamp tag with overlapping lime and sunflower flowers. Stamp orchid "just for you" in center; ink edges of tag with orchid ink pad. Knot ribbon through hole in tag. Insert tag in pocket. ■

SOURCES: Card from Die Cuts With A View; printed paper and fabric pocket from K&Company; flower stamp from Hero Arts; chalk ink from Tsukineko Inc.; ribbon from May Arts; tape from Therm O Web.

Petals & Peeps

DESIGN BY KATHLEEN PANEITZ

Pocket: Adhere a 4¼ x 2½-inch piece of printed paper to front of pocket with bottom edges even. Attach daisy trim to front of pocket over edge of printed paper, attaching a mini brad through the center of each flower. Tie ribbon around pocket; fold out ribbon ends at an angle and trim on the diagonal. Adhere flower charm over ribbon as shown in photo. Apply rub-on transfer to pocket.

Tag: Center and adhere a 1½-inch square of printed paper at top edge of tag. Attach brass ring hanger over top of tag with mini brads. ■

SOURCES: Pocket with tag card, rub-on transfers and flower charm from Making Memories; printed paper from Sassafras Lass.

MATERIALS

4¼ x 5¼-inch light blue pocket with white tag card

Orange/white/blue chicks-and-flowers printed paper

"happy Easter" rub-on transfer

White-and-blue enameled flower charm

8 light blue mini brads

Brass ring hanger

⁷⁄₁₆-inch-wide yellow grosgrain ribbon

⅝-inch-wide white daisy trim

Adhesive lines *and* dots

I am so grateful!
Thanks so very much!

thank you

So Grateful

DESIGN BY SUSAN COBB, COURTESY OF HOT OFF THE PRESS

MATERIALS

5 x 6½-inch white card

Printed papers: pink,
dark pink, pink linen,
pink diamonds, pink/
yellow/lime stripes,
sponged yellow

Card-stock stickers: "thank
you" quotations, pink/
yellow/lime flowers
and tags

Black ink pad

⅜-inch-wide white-on-pink
polka-dot ribbon

Brads: ¼-inch yellow, ⅛-inch
yellow and deep pink

Templates: pocket, tag

Paper piercer *or* large
needle

Paper glue

Mini adhesive dots

Adhesive foam tape

Adhere a 5 x 6½-inch piece of pink diamonds printed paper to front of card. Adhere a 5 x ½-inch strip of sponged yellow paper across front of card with top edge 2½ inches from top of card. Adhere a 5 x 1-inch strip of striped printed paper (with stripes running vertically) over yellow strip, leaving ⅛-inch yellow border visible. Adhere a 5 x 2½-inch piece of pink linen paper across top of card with edges even. Ink outer edges of card.

Cut out quotations; ink edges. Adhere larger quotation to dark pink paper cut slightly larger than quote; ink edges. Fold a 1½-inch piece of ribbon in half to form tab; center tab along left edge of matted quotation and adhere on reverse side with mini adhesive dots. Adhere quotation to top portion of card.

Adhere square flower sticker to card front over striped border with foam tape. Attach yellow brad through center of flower and card front.

Using templates, trace pocket onto striped paper; trace tag shape onto pink linen paper and cut out. Adhere sponged yellow paper to back of pocket, trimming edges even.

Ink edges of pink linen tag. Ink edges of small pink tag sticker; attach to top edge of pink linen tag with deep pink brad. Adhere small "thank you" quotation over tags as shown. Adhere tag inside pocket; adhere pocket to card. Tie ribbon in a bow; adhere over right edge of pocket as shown with mini adhesive dots.

Inside card: Cut a 5 x 2½-inch piece of diamonds printed paper; ink edges and adhere strip across center of card. Ink edges of a 2 x 1⅛-inch pink paper tag sticker; attach ribbon tab to left end using ⅛-inch yellow brad. Adhere tag to pink diamonds paper and flower square sticker over top edge of pink diamonds strip. ■

SOURCE: Cardmaker's Citrus Creative Pack printed papers and card-stock stickers, Citrus ribbon and thank-you quotations from Hot Off The Press.

May the beautiful
memories that fill
your heart help to
bring you comfort.

WITH *Sympathy*

Comfort Your Heart

DESIGN BY LISA JOHNSON

Pocket: Score and fold a 4¼ x 11-inch piece of green card stock in half to form a 4¼ x 5½-inch pocket. Round corners along open edge using corner rounder punch. Score across pocket front 1¼ inches from top; fold down.

Open pocket; stamp front of flap and inside of card above flap with dark blue floral background. Stamp and shadow-stamp green leaves-and-berries motif on pocket front in lower right corner. Ink pocket edges with green ink.

Punch two ½-inch circles from dark blue card stock and two ¼-inch circles from green card stock; ink circles with matching inks. Attach circles and mini brads to front of pocket as shown in photo; wrap jute twine between mini brads.

Adhere adhesive mini dots inside upper corners of pocket flap as close to edge as possible; press to close.

Pocket panel: Ink edges of a 3⅛ x 1½-inch piece of dark blue card stock with dark blue ink; round corners using corner rounder punch. Stamp green leaves-and-berries motif once onto scrap paper, then shadow-stamp image onto off-white card stock. Stamp dark blue "WITH Sympathy" over leaves and berries. Trim to 2⅞ x 1¼ inches; round corners using corner rounder punch and adhere to blue card stock, over flap near right-hand edge.

Tag card: Cut a 3¼ x 5-inch piece from off-white card stock and a 3½ x 5¼-inch piece from dark blue card stock; round upper corners of both pieces using corner rounder punch. Stamp and shadow-stamp green leaves-and-berries motif off right edge of off-white card stock; ink edges with green ink. Center and stamp dark blue sentiment on card stock 1⅛ inches from top edge. Ink dark blue card stock with dark blue ink. Center and adhere stamped off-white card stock to dark blue card stock.

Punch a 1¼-inch circle from dark blue card stock and a ½-inch circle from green card stock; ink with matching colors of ink. Fold dark blue circle in half over top edge of tag card; center green circle on front. Adhere layers with adhesive mini dots. Punch ¹⁄₁₆-inch hole through all layers; set mini brad in hole. ■

SOURCE: Rubber stamps from Stampin' Up!

MATERIALS

Card stock: green, dark blue, off-white
Rubber stamps: "WITH Sympathy," sympathetic sentiment, leaves-and-berries motif, floral background
Ink pads: green, dark blue
3 "antique" copper mini brads
Jute twine
Punches: corner rounder, ¹⁄₁₆-inch hole, 1¼-inch circle,. ½-inch circle, ¼-inch circle
Adhesive mini dots

Autumn Splendor

DESIGN BY KRIS SMITH

MATERIALS

Striped printed paper in
    autumn colors
Card-stock stickers in
    autumn colors: banners,
    ribbons, words
2⅜ x 4¾-inch manila tag
⅜-inch-wide green-on-
    green polka-dot ribbon
4 copper eyelet snaps
³⁄₁₆-inch hole punch
Adhesive foam dots
Glue

Pocket: Cut one piece of striped paper 3⅜ x 5 inches and another piece 3⅜ inches square. Lay smaller piece on larger piece with bottom and side edges even. Punch a hole through both layers in each corner of the smaller piece. Set copper eyelet snaps in holes.

Cut small "AUTUMN" from ribbon stickers; refer to photo for placement and adhere. Cut a 3⅜-inch strip of thin green ribbon from ribbon stickers; adhere as shown.

Cut a 3⅜ x ¼-inch strip from multistriped ribbon sticker; adhere as shown. Cut a 3⅜ x ½-inch strip from maroon-and-white ribbon sticker; adhere as shown. Adhere a 3⅜ x ¼-inch strip of gold ribbon sticker over maroon-and-white sticker; adhere a 3⅜ x ⅛-inch strip of maroon ribbon sticker over gold ribbon sticker as shown.

Cut a single rectangle around the words "BONFIRE," "BOUNTY" and "GOLD" from banner stickers; adhere to right side of pocket front as shown.

Cut "CRACKLE" from ribbon border stickers; adhere over word panel using foam dots. Cut "LEAVES" rectangle from ribbon border stickers; adhere as shown.

Tag: Adhere red leaf sticker from banner stickers to tag 1¼ inches from top edge (with hole). Below red leaf sticker, adhere the following in order, edge to edge: 2⅜ x ⅛-inch green ribbon sticker, 2⅜ x ½-inch "AUTUMN" sticker, 2⅜ x ⅛-inch maroon ribbon sticker, 2⅜ x ¼-inch striped ribbon sticker, and 2⅜ x ⅛-inch green ribbon sticker.

Adhere 5-inch strips of ⅛-inch-wide gold ribbon stickers up edges of tag; trim even with edges.

At top of tag, adhere a 2⅜ x ⅝-inch strip of maroon-and-white striped ribbon sticker as shown; adhere "SPLENDOR" rectangle to maroon-and-white ribbon.

Cut two ½-inch-square images from ribbon sticker; adhere to top of tag on each side of hole. Thread ribbon through hole. Insert tag into pocket. ∎

SOURCE: Printed paper, stickers and eyelet snaps from Cloud 9 Design.

Enjoy Autumn

DESIGN BY DAWN MOORE

MATERIALS

Rust textured card stock

Striped printed paper in autumn colors

Autumn quotations card-stock stickers

Brown chalk ink

¼-inch wide brown/beige gingham-checked ribbon

Silk autumn leaf

Label maker with black adhesive label tape

Stapler with silver staples

Glue

Pocket: Cut a 6-inch square of card stock and a 6 x 3-inch piece of printed paper with stripes running vertically. Ink edges of both pieces. Staple printed paper to card stock along sides and bottom to form pocket.

Referring to photo for placement, adhere a quotation sticker to lower right corner of pocket. Cut 4-inch and 4½-inch pieces of ribbon; knot together at one end, leaving 1-inch tails. Adhere across pocket with knot nearer right-hand edge. Trim ends even with sides of pocket.

Adhere silk leaf to left side of pocket. Type "ENJOY" and "AUTUMN" on separate strips of black label tape; adhere labels at an angle over leaf.

Tag card: Cut a 4¼ x 5-inch piece of rust card stock and trim corners to form tag. Cut 4¼ x 1-inch and 4¼ x ½-inch strips of printed paper with stripes running vertically. Adhere 1-inch-wide strip across bottom of tag, and ½-inch-wide strip across top of tag.

Adhere a quotation sticker to center of tag. Fold a 4½-inch strip of ribbon into a V and staple to top of tag. Insert tag into pocket. ■

SOURCES: Printed paper from Scenic Route Paper Co. Inc.; ink from Clearsnap Inc.; ribbon from May Arts.

Happy Bird-day to You

DESIGN BY EMILY CALL, COURTESY OF STAMPIN' UP!

Form a 5½ x 4¼-inch top-fold card from kraft card stock.

Stamp surface of three-window card-stock pocket with canvas background stamp and caramel ink. Assemble pocket; adhere to front of card with opening at right side.

Cut a 4¾ x 2⁵⁄₁₆-inch rectangle from confetti white card stock and insert into pocket. Ink bird stamps with brush end of markers; stamp bird images onto card stock through windows.

Remove stamped card stock, punch a hole in right-hand edge and set eyelet in hole. Thread ribbon through eyelet and reposition rectangle in pocket.

Ink "happy bird-day to you!" stamp with black marker; stamp front of card below lower right corner of pocket. ■

SOURCE: Card stock, pocket, stamps, ink pad, markers and eyelet from Stampin' Up!

MATERIALS

Confetti white card-stock
  3-window pocket
Card stock: kraft, confetti
  white
Rubber stamps: canvas
  background, birds, "happy
  bird-day to you!"
Caramel ink pad
Markers with brush tips:
  olive green, orange, red,
  teal, turquoise, black
Orange eyelet
6mm red-and-white
  gingham-checked ribbon
⅛-inch hole punch
Eyelet-setting tool
Glue

SHAKER CARDS

Seed beads, glitter, paper confetti shapes,
tiny jingle bells—any diminutive decorative item
can be stashed behind the window of a shaker
card. Adding a bit of noise and a lot of movement
will delight recipients of any age.

Delivering Love

DESIGN BY LISA JOHNSON

Center and stamp a dark pink envelope image on 2½ x 2-inch and 2⅜ x 1⅞-inch pieces of shimmery white card stock.

Trim out bottom portion of envelope on larger piece, cutting inside stamped lines. Adhere a 2⅜ x 1⅞-inch piece of transparency to back of card stock using double-sided tape. Thread ribbon through two holes punched in upper left corner of card stock; knot on front and trim ends.

Adhere strips of foam tape around edge of smaller piece of card stock to create a box around stamped image. Make sure there are no gaps in the tape. Pour micro beads into box formed by foam tape. Adhere window over bottom of shaker.

Center and adhere shaker box to 2⁵⁄₁₆ x 2¼-inch black card stock rectangle using mini adhesive dots.

Adhere shaker box to a 3⅛ x 3¹⁄₁₆-inch rectangle of hot pink card stock at an angle using mini adhesive dots. Stamp black "delivering love" in lower right corner.

Adhere shaker box panel to card at an angle using mini adhesive dots. ∎

SOURCES: Card stock, stamps and micro beads from Stampin' Up!; card from A Muse Artstamps.

MATERIALS

- 4¼-inch-square black-and-white note card
- Card stock: hot pink, black, shimmery white
- Transparency sheet
- Rubber stamps: envelope, "delivering love"
- Dye ink pads: dark pink, black
- Clear micro beads
- Iridescent ultrafine glitter
- ³⁄₁₆-inch-wide black-and-white ribbon
- Craft knife
- Double hole punch
- Mini adhesive dots
- Adhesive foam tape

MATERIALS

Black textured card stock

Red tone-on-tone printed
  paper: tic-tac-toe, XO

3-inch black flower die cut

Premade shaker boxes: "be
  mine" oval, heart-with-
  arrow circle

Double-sided tape

Glue

Be Mine

DESIGN BY TAMI MAYBERRY

Form a 4 x 6-inch card from black card stock. Adhere a 3¾ x 5¾-inch rectangle of XO printed paper to front of card.

Adhere a 4 x 1-inch strip of black card stock ½ inch from bottom edge. Adhere a 4 x ¾-inch strip of tic-tac-toe printed paper to black card-stock strip. Adhere premade "be mine" oval shaker to strip.

Adhere a 2⅜ x 2⅞-inch piece of tic-tac-toe printed paper to 2½ x 3-inch black card-stock rectangle and attach to card front. Adhere black flower die cut over printed paper rectangle; adhere circle shaker box to center of flower. ■

SOURCES: Printed papers and shaker boxes from Carolee's Creations; flower die cut from Deluxe Designs.

Look Who's 40

DESIGN BY TAMI MAYBERRY

Form a 4 x 6-inch card from black card stock.

Tear off the bottom left corner of a 3½ x 5½-inch piece of black card stock and adhere to a 3¾ x 5¾-inch piece of black squares printed paper.

Thread black twill tape onto ends of "Happy Birthday" slide; staple ends of tape at edges of printed paper/card-stock panel, near bottom. Adhere a 2 x ½-inch strip of gray card stock to panel behind slide.

Cut two 2-inch squares from striped printed paper; ink edges with black ink. Adhere squares to printed paper/card-stock panel at an angle as shown.

Shaker: Adhere the precut shaker to a 2½-inch square of black card stock. Fill the shaker with "40" birthday confetti. Cover with precut transparency square and black foam top. Apply alphabet rub-on transfers to spell "Look who's 40" on top of shaker box.

Adhere shaker box to printed paper/card-stock panel. Adhere assembled panel to front of card. ■

SOURCES: Printed Papers from We R Memory Keepers; shaker box kit from Idea Tool Box/Advantus Corp.; birthday ribbon slide from All My Memories; rub-on transfers from Royal & Langnickel.

MATERIALS

Card stock: black textured, gray

Black/white/gray printed papers: concentric squares, stripes

Square black foam shaker box kit

Silver-and-black alphabet rub-on transfers

Black ink pad

"Happy Birthday" ribbon slide

½-inch-wide black twill tape

"40th birthday" confetti

Stapler with silver staples

Double-sided tape *or* glue

Jingle All the Way

DESIGN BY MARY AYRES

MATERIALS

White card stock

Squares printed paper:
green, red

4-inch-diameter ¼-inch-
thick circle shaker shape

Jingle bells phrases rub-on
transfers

35–40 (³⁄₁₆-inch) gold jingle
bells

⅝-inch-wide satin ribbon:
green, red

1½-inch-wide sheer gold
metallic ribbon

Instant-dry paper glue

Form a 5 x 8-inch card from card stock.

Cut 4¼ x 7¼-inch pieces from green and red printed papers. Adhere printed paper to front of card as shown in photo.

Adhere the precut self-adhesive foam shaker shape to front of card toward top and fill with jingle bells. Cover with precut transparency circle and white foam top. Tie a knot in the center of an 8-inch piece of gold metallic ribbon. Trim ends; adhere knot to top of shaker.

Apply jingle bells rub-on transfer to red satin ribbon. Apply second rub-on transfer to green satin ribbon. Wrap ribbons across bottom of card as shown, adhering ends to inside and back of card. ■

SOURCES: Printed paper from KI Memories; shaker shape from Idea Tool Box/Advantus Corp.; rub-on transfers from Royal & Langnickel; glue from Beacon.

happy holidays

Sugarplum Snowman

DESIGN BY BETSY EDWARDS, COURTESY OF ROYAL & LANGNICKEL

Apply snowman-with-candy rub-on transfer to card, positioning it inside window opening. Apply gumdrop rub-on transfers to card front as desired. Using craft stick, apply a very thin layer of glue to card front. Shake iridescent glitter onto wet glue; tap off excess. Let dry.

Fill bubble front with beads and candy embellishments and assemble card according to manufacturer's instructions.

Apply "happy holidays" rub-on transfer inside card. Embellish envelope as desired. ∎

SOURCES: Card, envelope, bubble front and rub-on transfers from Royal & Langnickel; embellishments from Jesse James & Co.

MATERIALS

5 x 6⅞-inch card with oval window opening

Envelope to fit 5 x 6⅞-inch card

Oval bubble front

Glittery rub-on transfers: snowman with candy, gumdrops, candy canes, lollipops

"happy holidays" rub-on transfer

3 candy embellishments

Clear E beads

Multicolored seed beads

Iridescent white glitter

Craft stick

Paper adhesive

MATERIALS

Lavender textured card
    stock

Printed paper

2-inch-square purple
    cellophane self-sealing
    envelope

¼-inch alphabet rubber
    stamps

Purple dye ink pad

Assorted sequins: purple,
    blue, green, yellow

Adhesive foam tape

Thinking of You

DESIGN BY SUSAN HUBER

Form a 4¼ x 5½-inch card from lavender card stock. Ink edges with ink pad.

Cut a 2-inch square of printed paper; insert into cellophane envelope. Add sequins, close envelope and seal. Adhere to card 1⅛ inches from top with foam tape.

Stamp "thinking of you" onto front of card below envelope. ∎

SOURCE: Rubber stamps from Hero Arts.

MATERIALS

6 x 4-inch white greeting card
with oval cutout for use
with bubble front

Pastel textured card stock:
yellow, pink, green, lavender

Magenta card stock

Oval bubble front

Magenta ink pad

Rub-on transfers: retro circles,
light blue alphabet and stars

Scraps of ¼- to ⅜-inch-wide
satin ribbons: pink, light
green, lavender

Quilling tool

Standard office-style paper
punch

Paper piercer or large needle

¼-inch-wide double-sided tape

Congrats

DESIGN BY KAREN DESMET

Apply retro circle rub-on transfers to card, positioning them inside window opening. Apply light blue stars and alphabet rub-on transfers to spell "Congrats" to bubble front.

Cut 18–24 strips 3 x ½ inch from assorted pastel card stocks; curl into tight coils using quilling tool. Punch 10–15 circles from magenta card stock using standard paper punch.

Fill bubble front with quilled coils and punched circles and assemble card following manufacturer's instructions.

Ink edges of card with ink pad. Using a paper piercer or large needle, punch three pairs of holes evenly spaced down left edge of card front. Thread ribbons through holes; knot and trim ends. ■

SOURCES: Card and bubble front from Royal & Langnickel; rub-on transfers from Scrapworks; tape from Therm O Web.

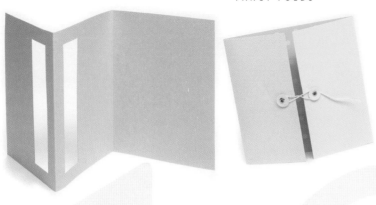

FANCY FOLDS

Tired of the same old fold-on-the-left-side routine? Embrace the unusual when you experiment with tea-bag folding, iris folding and cards that fold anyplace except where you expect!

Bundle of Boy

DESIGN BY HEATHER D. WHITE

Adhere two 2⅛ x 5½-inch pieces of blue paisley printed paper to rectangular areas of card's front panels. Cut triangles of striped paper to fit front flaps; adhere.

Adhere left half only of baby boy embellishment to left-hand triangular flap. ■

SOURCES: Printed papers from Bo-Bunny Press; baby boy embellishment from me & my BIG ideas.

4¼ x 5½-inch card with
bifold front panels and
triangular front flaps
Printed papers: blue paisley,
blue/green/white stripes
Baby boy embellishment
Paper adhesive

True Friend

MATERIALS

Red card stock

Red stripe/solid lime double-sided printed paper

Friendship-themed card-stock stickers

Red distress ink

2 red heart eyelets

Eyelet-setting tool

Corner rounder punch

Paper adhesive

DESIGN BY LINDA BEESON

Cut an 11¾ x 5¾-inch piece of printed paper. Score printed paper vertically 3¼ inches from right-hand edge and 3 inches from left-hand edge to form three-panel card. Fold sides toward center with left-hand panel on top. Round corners of overlapping panels with corner rounder punch. Ink edges of card.

Ink edges and surfaces of "true" and "friend" stickers; mount on red card-stock rectangles cut slightly larger all around. Attach stickers to front of card with heart eyelets as shown in photo, positioning stickers ¼ inch apart and overlapping card opening; left edges of stickers are 1½ inches from left-hand fold.

Inside card: Ink "memories" sticker; mount on red card-stock rectangle cut slightly larger all around. Center and adhere inside card. ■

SOURCES: Printed paper and card-stock stickers from My Mind's Eye; ink from Ranger Industries.

I Love You Forever

DESIGN BY DAWN MOORE

Cut a 12 x 5-inch piece of printed card stock. Score card stock vertically 2½ inches from left-hand edge and fold toward center; re-open. Fold right-hand side toward center to first fold line and crease, forming a 5 x 4¾-inch gatefold card. Ink all edges.

Ink edges of "I love you!" and brown circle punch-outs. Referring to photo for placement throughout, set an eyelet in the lower right corner of "I love you!" punch-out and adhere to left-hand flap of card.

Attach pink paper flower to brown circle punch-out with black mini brad; adhere to card front.

Set an eyelet in the right-hand flap of the card. Referring to inset photo, thread ribbon through eyelets. Ink edges of "forever" punch-out and a 4¾ x 4½-inch piece of cream card stock; center and adhere to inside panel, "trapping" ribbon. Close card; tie ribbon ends in a bow on front. ∎

SOURCE: Printed card stock and punch-outs from Colorbök.

MATERIALS

Card stock: printed green/
   cream/brown circles, solid
   cream
Punch-outs: "forever," "I love
   you!," brown circle
Black chalk ink
⅝-inch pink paper flower
Black mini brad
2 pink eyelets
⅛-inch-wide pink-and-white
   pin-dot ribbon
Eyelet-setting tool
Paper adhesive

Joy in the Journey

DESIGN BY HEATHER D. WHITE

MATERIALS

- 5-inch-square tan card with tab-and-slot closure
- Printed papers: pink-on-pink, pink/lavender/white floral
- Pink flower card-stock sticker
- 3⅜ x 2⅜-inch photo
- "the Joy is in the Journey" rub-on transfer
- Brown paper stain
- Craft knife
- Paper adhesive

Position card with fold at left. Ink edges of a 4 x 5-inch piece of floral printed paper and adhere to front of card. Cut slots in printed paper with craft knife.

Ink edges of a 2 x 5-inch piece of pink-on-pink printed paper; adhere inside card, ½ inch from right-hand edge.

Center and adhere photo to a 4 x 2⅝-inch piece of pink-on-pink printed paper; ink edges and adhere to front of card ⅝ inch from top edge.

Lightly ink all remaining tan edges of card.

Apply rub-on transfer to card front above photo. Lightly ink edges of card-stock sticker; adhere to card, overlapping lower left corner of photo. ∎

SOURCES: Card from Making Memories; printed papers and card-stock sticker from Designs by Reminisce; rub-on transfer from All My Memories.

Sweet & Sassy

DESIGN BY KATHLEEN PANEITZ

Project note: *Adhere elements using paper adhesive unless instructed otherwise.*

Cover front panel of card with flowers printed paper; cover flap with gingham printed paper.

Using paper glaze, adhere transparent letters near bottom edge of card to spell "hi." Knot ribbon around clip; slide clip over top of card. ∎

SOURCES: Card from K&Company; printed papers from Provo Craft and Bo-Bunny Press; clip from Junkitz; transparent letters from Autumn Leaves; paper glaze from Duncan Enterprises.

MATERIALS

4¼ x 5½-inch card with
   curved flap closure
Printed papers: orange-and-
   white gingham-checked,
   orange/pink/white flowers
3-inch pink transparent
   letters to spell "hi"
"Sweet & Sassy" pink clip
⅝-inch-wide pink-and-white
   striped ribbon
Paper glaze
Paper adhesive

Dreaming of Spring

DESIGN BY ALICE GOLDEN

Cut a 9¼ x 3⅝-inch piece of snowflake circles printed paper into two pieces to fit on each side of card front, and adhere.

Cut two 3⅝ x 1-inch strips from the same printed paper; turn over and stack with edges even. Punch three evenly spaced ¼-inch holes down center of strips and adhere to card front on both sides of center opening, ⅛ inch from edge.

Using holes in strips as a guide, punch holes through front panels of card. Thread ribbons through pairs of holes; knot ribbons to close card.

Punch tag from snowflakes blocks printed paper and apply rub-on transfer. Tie tag to one of the ribbon ties with silver metallic thread. ■

SOURCES: Card from Die Cuts With A View; printed papers from Scenic Route Paper Co.; rub-on transfer from BasicGrey; ribbons from American Crafts; tag punch from QuicKutz Inc.

MATERIALS

9¼ x 3⅞-inch red textured gatefold card

Reversible snowflakes printed papers: red/pink/turquoise/lime circles and blocks

Winter-themed rub-on transfer

Printed ribbons: stripe, diagonal stripe, circles

Silver metallic thread

Punches: 1³⁄₁₆ x 1⁷⁄₁₆-inch tag, ¼-inch hole

Glue stick

Touched by Friendship

DESIGN BY HEATHER D. WHITE

Score and fold a 12 x 3-inch strip of card stock every 3 inches to form a four-panel accordion-fold card.

Cut four 3-inch squares of diamonds printed paper; adhere to panels of card. Embellish panels with strips cut from other printed papers and card-stock stickers. ■

SOURCE: Printed papers and card-stock stickers from Bo-Bunny Press.

MATERIALS

Green card stock

Printed papers: red/green/cream stripes, green-on-green diamonds, red-and-white checks

Friends-themed card-stock stickers

Paper adhesive

North Woods Greeting

DESIGN BY LISA JOHNSON

Project note: *Adhere elements using paper adhesive unless instructed otherwise.*

Cut three 4⅜-inch circles from rust card stock, one 2⅜-inch circle from brown, and one 1⅞-inch circle from ivory. Ink edges of all circles with brown ink.

Top panel: Randomly stamp rust circle with brown and rust pinecones and olive green pine needles. Stamp a brown pinecone and olive green pine needles in center of the ivory circle. Punch an even number of 1/16-inch holes around edge of ivory circle; thread hemp twine through holes like a running stitch and adhere ends on reverse side.

Center and adhere brown circle to stamped rust circle, then adhere ivory circle using foam squares.

Center panel: Stamp two olive green trees on rust circle, stamping each tree twice for a shadowed effect. Stamp brown geese and brown "Thinking of you" over trees.

Bottom panel: Center 2¾-inch circle template from journaling lines stamp set on rust circle. Stamp brown journaling lines within circle; sponge brown ink lightly over stamped lines. Mask journaling lines with scrap-paper circle cut using same template; stamp brown pinecones and olive green needles around edges.

Assembly: Referring to photo, sandwich layers together and punch ⅛-inch holes as shown. Set mini brads through top hole of top panel and bottom hole of bottom panel; knot hemp twine around brads. Set remaining mini brads in holes as shown in photo to connect the circles. Card will rotate open when ends of hemp are pulled. ■

SOURCE: Rubber stamps from Stampin' Up!

MATERIALS

Card stock: brown, rust, ivory

Rubber stamps: tree, pinecone, pine needles, geese, "thinking of you," journaling lines with 2¾-inch circle template

Dye ink pads: olive green, brown, rust

4 silver mini brads

Fine hemp twine

Hole punches: 1/16-inch, ⅛-inch

Circle templates: 4⅜-inch, 2⅜-inch, 1⅞-inch

Paper adhesive

Adhesive foam mounting squares

Sweet Treats

DESIGN BY LINDA BEESON

MATERIALS

Card stock: orange, black,
 purple, white

Black/orange/purple/lime
 printed papers: polka
 dots, stripes

Rubber stamps: candy corn,
 "Trick or Treat"

Black ink pad

Clear embossing powder

Watercolor crayons

Crystal lacquer

4 orange snaps

Embossing heat tool

Circle punches: 1½-inch,
 1¾-inch, 1⅞-inch

Paper adhesive

Adhesive foam tape

Project note: *Adhere elements using paper adhesive unless instructed otherwise.*

Card base: Center and adhere a 5-inch square of polka-dot printed paper to a 5¼-inch square of orange card stock. Set orange snap in each corner.

Mini card: Form a 3-inch-square card from orange card stock. Position fold on left edge; center and adhere mini card to card base.

Center and adhere a 2⅝-inch square of striped printed paper to a 2¾-inch square of black card stock; center and adhere to front of mini card.

Stamp candy corn image on a 1½-inch circle punched from white card stock; sprinkle clear embossing powder on ink and heat with embossing tool until powder melts. Color candies with watercolor crayons; coat candies only with crystal lacquer.

Center and adhere white circle to a 1¾-inch black circle, then to a 1⅞-inch purple circle. Center and adhere circles to mini card with foam tape.

Stamp "Trick or Treat" on a 1¾-inch circle punched from white card stock. Center and adhere white circle to a 1⅞-inch purple circle; center and adhere inside mini card. ■

SOURCES: Printed paper from Creative Imaginations; rubber stamps from Paper Salon; crystal lacquer from Sakura Hobby Craft.

MATERIALS

Tea bag in foil packet

Card stock: light blue, blue

Rubber stamps: snowflakes wheel stamp, "Holiday Greetings"

Ink: light blue, white pigment, dark blue pigment

¼-inch-wide blue grosgrain ribbon

Fine silver metallic cord

Glitter

Punches: snowflake, ⅛-inch hole, 1¼-inch circle, 1⅜-inch circle

Stapler

Paper adhesive

Glitzy Holiday Greetings

DESIGN BY LISA JOHNSON

Cut a 3 x 8½-inch piece of blue card stock. Score card stock horizontally 1¼ inches from top edge and 3½ inches from bottom edge.

Stamp both sides of card stock with light blue snowflakes. Apply white pigment ink to edges using a gentle, sweeping motion.

Sandwich edge of tea bag under narrower fold at top; staple through all layers at center to attach tea bag. Tie ribbon and silver cord around top fold, concealing staple. Fold up bottom panel; stamp front of card with dark blue "Holiday Greetings."

Snowflake tag: Punch a 1¼-inch circle from light blue card stock and a 1⅜-inch circle from blue card stock. Punch a snowflake in center of light blue circle. Coat center of blue circle with adhesive, avoiding edges. Press light blue circle onto blue circle; sprinkle with glitter; tap off excess.

Punch a ⅛-inch hole through tag near edge; cut slit from edge to hold. Slide tag onto silver cord at top of card; tie cord to ribbon and adhere tag to ribbon. ■

SOURCE: Rubber stamps from Stampin' Up!

MATERIALS

Pink textured card stock

Springtime text printed paper

Stickers: 1⁷⁄₁₆-inch-square
  flower, transparent "Smiles
  are springing up all over"

³⁄₈-inch-wide pink ribbon

Small silver safety pin

Silver jump ring

Stapler with staples

Paper adhesive

Adhesive dots

Smiles Are Springing Up

DESIGN BY JEANNE WYNHOFF

Project note: *Adhere elements with paper adhesive unless instructed otherwise.*

Score horizontally across a 4¼ x 11¼-inch piece of card stock 1 inch from bottom edge; fold up to form bottom tab. Staple across bottom tab ¼ inch from fold.

Score across card stock 4¾ inches from top edge; fold down and tuck into bottom flap, forming a 4¼ x 5½-inch card.

Cut a 7-inch piece of ribbon in half and knot ends together. Adhere to a 4⅛ x 4¼-inch piece of printed paper 2 inches from top with knot slightly to right of center. Wrap ends to reverse side and tape. Center and adhere printed paper to front of card ¹⁄₁₆ inch from top and side edges.

Adhere card-stock sticker to card stock and trim, leaving a narrow border. Poke hole through corner of sticker; attach jump ring and thread onto safety pin. Pin sticker to ribbon knot. Adhere sticker to front of card with adhesive dots. Adhere transparent sticker to bottom flap. ■

SOURCES: Printed paper from Pressed Petals; card-stock sticker from O'Scrap; transparent sticker from EK Success Ltd.

School Photos Folder

DESIGN BY JEANNE WYNHOFF

MATERIALS

Dark blue textured card
   stock
Red-on-red checked printed
   paper
Stickers: card-stock
   "SCHOOL," 1½-inch
   alphabet
⅜-inch numeral rubber
   stamps
Black pigment ink
Stapler with staples
Paper adhesive

Score horizontally across a 4¼ x 11¼-inch piece of card stock 1 inch from bottom edge; fold up to form bottom tab. Staple across bottom tab ½ inch from fold.

Score across card stock 4¾ inches from top edge; fold down and tuck into bottom flap, forming a 4¼ x 5½-inch card.

Ink edges of a 4⅛ x 4¼-inch piece of printed paper; adhere to front of card ¹⁄₁₆ inch from top and side edges. Staple paper randomly along bottom edge on right-hand side.

Adhere a 3¾ x 1⅝-inch piece of card stock to upper left corner of card as shown in photo.

Adhere card-stock sticker to card stock and trim, leaving a narrow border. Adhere panel to printed paper and trim, leaving a narrow border. Adhere panel to card as shown in photo.

Attach stickers to spell "PHOTOS." Stamp year in lower left corner. Randomly staple edges of card-stock sticker. ∎

SOURCES: Printed paper from Daisy D's Paper Co.; card-stock sticker from O'Scrap; alphabet stickers from Sticker Studio.

Friendship
lightens every
burden and
makes the sun
shine
brighter.

MATERIALS

4¼ x 5½-inch pink
matchbook-style card
base with scalloped edge

Yellow card stock

Printed papers: citrus
stripes, pink/orange plaid

Transparent friendship-
themed sticker

Pink jumbo rickrack

Paper adhesive

Adhesive dots

Friendship Lightens Every Burden

DESIGN BY STACEY STAMITOLES

Project note: *Adhere elements with paper adhesive unless instructed otherwise.*

Adhere a 4¼ x 4⁵⁄₁₆-inch piece of striped printed paper to top panel of card. Trim 4¼ x 1½-inch piece of plaid printed paper to match scalloped edge of card flap and adhere. Adhere rickrack across bottom flap.

Adhere transparent sticker to plaid printed paper; trim around sticker. Adhere panel to card stock; trim, leaving a ⅛-inch border. Center and adhere panel to card with adhesive dots ⁷⁄₁₆ inch from top fold. ■

SOURCES: Card and sticker from Die Cuts With A View; printed papers from Frances Meyer Inc.

On Safari

DESIGN BY SUSAN STRINGFELLOW

Lightly ink surfaces and edges of card. Adhere a 4-inch square of printed paper to large flap of card as shown in photo.

Stamp elephant onto card stock; trim around stamped image. Wrap hemp cord around bottom of stamped image; knot ends near right edge, tying on glass leaf charm. Adhere to card near left edge.

Adhere twill tape across scalloped top panel, near top edge. Center and attach black mini brads through ends of twill tape. Stamp "SAFARI" on twill tape near right-hand edge. ■

SOURCES: Card base from Die Cuts With A View; printed paper from The Paper Co.; rubber stamps from Sugarloaf Products.

MATERIALS

4¼ x 5½-inch tan matchbook-style card base with scalloped edge

Light tan textured card stock

Animal prints printed paper

Rubber stamps: "SAFARI," elephant

Black pigment ink

Green glass leaf charm

2 black mini brads

Fine hemp twine

⅝-inch-wide off-white twill tape

Paper adhesive

Filled With Love

DESIGN BY SUSAN COBB, COURTESY OF HOT OFF THE PRESS

MATERIALS

6½ x 5-inch card

Printed papers: aqua linen, aqua/lime stripe, aqua dots

Blue paper blank label

Birthday quotations

Black ink pad

3 black photo turn mounts

Mini brads: 5 lime green, 2 black

⅜-inch-wide lime green grosgrain ribbon

¹⁄₁₆-inch hole punch

Paper adhesive

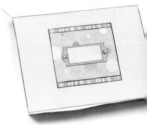

Open card and lay flat with inner surface facing up. Score horizontally across card 1⅜ inches from bottom edge; fold bottom up to create bottom flap. Score across card 3¾ inches from top edge; fold down to create top flap.

Adhere a 6½ x 3¾-inch piece of dots printed paper to top flap. Ink edges. Adhere a 6½ x 1⅜-inch piece of linen printed paper to bottom flap. Ink edges. Ink edges of a 6½ x ½-inch strip of striped printed paper; center and adhere to bottom flap.

Trim rectangle around birthday quotation; ink edges. Adhere quotation to linen printed paper and trim, leaving a ⅛-inch border; ink edges. Tie ribbon in a bow. Referring to photo for placement, adhere ribbon tab and bow to reverse side of quotation panel.

Punch ¹⁄₁₆-inch holes in upper corners of quotation panel; set black brads in holes. Punch three ¹⁄₁₆-inch holes evenly spaced across bottom of top flap, ½ inch from edge. Attach photo mounts with lime green brads.

Ink edges of a 6½ x 4¾-inch piece of linen printed paper and adhere to center panel inside card. Ink edges of a 3¼ x 3-inch piece of striped printed paper. Ink edges of a 3¼ x 2½-inch piece of dots printed paper; center and adhere to striped printed paper.

Ink edges of blank label; center and adhere to printed paper panel. Punch ¹⁄₁₆-inch holes through ends of label; set lime green brads in holes. Center and adhere printed paper panel inside card. ■

SOURCE: Printed papers and birthday quotations from Hot Off The Press.

Matchbook Thanks

DESIGN BY STACEY STAMITOLES

Ink edges of a 3⅛ x 2-inch piece of printed paper. Center and adhere printed paper to a 3¾ x 4⅝-inch piece of card stock ⅜ inch from top edge. Adhere metal tile to printed paper and adhere paper/card-stock panel to front of card.

Ink edges as desired. Apply rub-on transfers to card stock as shown in photo.

Adhere pieces of ribbon across top and bottom edges of bottom flap. Punch ⅟16-inch hole in center of bottom flap; set mini brad in hole. ■

SOURCES: Card base, printed paper, rub-on transfer and metal tile from Making Memories; ink from Ranger Industries.

MATERIALS

4¼ x 5½-inch cream matchbook-style card base

Dusty rose card stock

Floral/cream printed paper

"Thanks [wink]" rub-on transfer

Silver mini brad

Light tan distress ink

1-inch-square metal flower tile

⅜-inch-wide light green jacquard ribbon

⅟16-inch hole punch

Adhesive

MATERIALS

Card stock: light brown, brown, off-white, orange

Rubber stamps: flower, blocks, asterisk, dots, "hello"

Ink pads: light brown, brown, yellow, orange

3 "antique" copper mini brads

¼-inch-wide taupe-and-white gingham-checked ribbon

Punches: ¼-inch square, ¹⁄₁₆-inch hole

Sponge

Paper adhesive

Harvest Hello

DESIGN BY LISA JOHNSON

Cut an 11 x 4¼-inch piece of brown card stock. Score card stock vertically 1 inch from right-hand edge and 4½ inches from left-hand edge. Fold panels toward center, forming a 5½ x 4¼-inch gatefold card. Ink card with brown ink.

Closure: Attach ends of two pieces of ribbon to card flaps with copper mini brads ⅝ inch from bottom edge; knot ribbon ends together and trim.

Stamp light brown blocks and dots in center of a 3⅛ x 2¼-inch piece of off-white card stock; stamp flower in yellow, asterisks in orange and "hello" in brown. Set mini brad in center of yellow flower. Ink edges of card stock with light brown ink.

Ink edges and surface of a 3½ x 2⅝-inch piece of light brown card stock with light brown ink. Center and adhere stamped off-white card stock to light brown card stock.

Ink a 3½ x 2⅜-inch piece of orange card stock with light brown ink. Adhere both panels as shown.

Punch ¼-inch squares from light brown, off-white and orange card stock; center and adhere to right-hand flap of card in a vertical row, beginning ⅜ inch from top edge. ∎

SOURCE: Rubber stamps from Stampin' Up!

Rustic Birthday Side-Fold

DESIGN BY LISA JOHNSON

Form a 5½ x 4¼-inch card from kraft card stock. Round corners along open edge using corner rounder punch; ink edges with all colors. Score and fold right-hand edge of card front toward center ¾ inch from right-hand edge; apply all ink colors to flaps. Punch slit in back of card to hold folded front edge; set brad in center of slit.

Randomly stamp light brown and green circles and squares on front of card. Adhere front flap to front of card.

Cut a 1¾ x 4¼-inch strip from green card stock; round upper and lower right-hand corners using corner rounder punch. Ink surface with green ink. Set brads in upper and lower left-hand corners. Adhere strip to card ⅜ inch from fold.

Stamp "Birthdays are the BEST" in center of a 1⁹⁄₁₆-inch square of kraft card stock; stamp sentiment again directly over it with brown ink. Ink edges with brown and light brown inks.

Ink edges and surface of a 1⅞-inch square of brown card stock with brown ink; center and adhere stamped square to brown square. Adhere squares to card, overlapping edge of green strip. ■

SOURCE: Rubber stamps from Stampin' Up!

MATERIALS
Card stock: kraft, green, brown
Rubber stamps: 1-inch circle, 1-inch square, "Birthdays are the BEST"
Ink pads: brown, green, light brown
3 "antique" brass mini brads
Fine hemp twine
Punches: corner rounder, slit punch, ¹⁄₁₆-inch hole
Adhesive lines and dots

DIE CUTS

Die cuts personalize your card making experience by cutting the patterned paper of your choice into what ever shape you choose for the ultimate in versatility. Die-cutters range in size from portable and palm-sized to computer-controlled units that let you create die cuts from any piece of art work.

Christmas Lights

DESIGN BY SUSAN HUBER

Project note: Adhere elements using paper adhesive unless instructed otherwise.

Form a 5½ x 4¼-inch top-fold card from red card stock.

Cut a 5½ x 2⅛-inch strip of white card stock. Attach a gold square brad through card stock near edge at each end, ⅝ inch from top.

Die-cut one Christmas tree light each from red, blue, green and yellow card stocks using die cutter; color screw ends with gold leafing pen. Adhere light bulbs to white card stock at angles with foam tape.

Tie ends of a 6½-inch piece of black cord around mini brads. Tuck cord behind light bulbs as shown; secure cord with dots of adhesive.

Adhere white card-stock strip to card ⅞ inch from fold. Stamp "Christmas magic" in lower right corner of card. ■

SOURCES: Rubber stamp from A Muse Artstamps; gold leafing pen from Krylon; die-cutting tool and die from QuicKutz Inc.

MATERIALS

Card stock: red, yellow, blue, green, white
"Christmas magic" rubber stamp
Black pigment ink
Gold leafing pen
2 square gold mini brads
Narrow black cord
Die-cutting tool with Christmas light die
Paper adhesive
Adhesive foam tape

MATERIALS

White card stock

2 x 4⅜-inch pink Christmas
   tree die cut

Gray felt-tip marker *or* pen
   (optional)

Black pen *or* rub-on
   transfers (optional)

3 inches ⅜-inch-wide lime
   pin-dot grosgrain ribbon

Sewing machine with white
   thread

Adhesive dots

Computer with color printer
   and desired font

Pink Christmas Tree

DESIGN BY REBECCA COOPER, COURTESY OF ANNA GRIFFIN INC.

On computer, create a 3 x 5-inch text box; change outline to gray. Referring to photo throughout for placement, set "merry christmas" in black, centering phrase below gray box. Print images onto right-hand half of card stock so that box outline is no less than ⅜ inch from top and right-hand edges.

Trim card stock to 7½ x 7¾ inches; score and fold down center to form a 3¾ x 7¾-inch card with text box centered on front, ⅜ inch from top edge. *Option: Add 3 x 5-inch box to card with gray felt-tip marker or pen. Add words with black pen or rub-on transfers.*

Machine-stitch around edges of die cut. Center die cut inside text box and adhere to card with adhesive dots. Knot center of ribbon; trim ribbon ends. Center and adhere knot to base of tree with adhesive dot. ■

SOURCE: Die cut from Anna Griffin Inc.

Christmas Joy

DESIGN BY SUSAN HUBER

Project note: *Adhere elements using paper adhesive unless instructed otherwise.*

Form a 4¼ x 5½-inch card from white card stock.

Ink side and top edges of a 4¼ x 4-inch piece of printed rustic card stock with gold leafing pen; adhere to card with top edges even.

Adhere a 1½ x 4¼-inch piece of gold card stock to bottom of card with bottom edges even. Adhere rickrack over seam. Stamp "joy" on printed card stock using red paint.

Die-cut two matching pairs of holly leaves from one green printed card stock. Adhere one pair directly to card over "j." Cut foam tape to fit on backs of remaining leaves; adhere directly on top of matching holly leaves. In the same way, add three holly berries around leaves, punching six ¼-inch circles from red card stock. Dot berries with glitter glue.

Die-cut two holly leaves from second green printed card stock; adhere to lower right corner of card. Adhere red buttons near leaves for holly berries. ∎

SOURCES: Card stock from Lasting Impressions and Bazzill; foam stamps from Making Memories; gold leafing pen from Krylon; die-cutting tool and dies from QuicKutz Inc.

MATERIALS

Card stock: plain white, gold
   textured, rustic white/
   gold dots print,
   2 green-on-green prints
2-inch foam alphabet
   stamps
Red acrylic craft paint
Red glitter glue
Gold leafing pen
3 tiny red buttons
Red rickrack
Die-cutting tool with holly
   leaf dies
¼-inch hole punch
Paper adhesive
Adhesive foam tape

Butterfly Thanks

DESIGN BY TAMI MAYBERRY

MATERIALS

Card stock: lilac, yellow

Printed papers: 1-inch blocks, flowers

Lavender butterfly die cut

½-inch-square lavender epoxy alphabet stickers

Paper adhesive

Form a 7 x 5-inch top-fold card from lilac card stock. Center and adhere a 6¾ x 4¾-inch piece of flowers printed paper to front of card.

Adhere a 6¾ x 1¼-inch strip of yellow card stock across card ¼ inch from bottom edge. Trim a strip of six squares from blocks printed paper; center and adhere to yellow strip. Adhere square epoxy letter stickers to blocks to spell "THANKS."

Center and adhere a 3¼ x 2¾-inch piece of yellow card stock to a 3½ x 3-inch piece of lilac card stock. Adhere lilac butterfly die cut to yellow card stock; center and adhere panel to card ⁵⁄₁₆ inch from fold. ■

SOURCES: Printed papers from Doodlebug Design Inc.; die cut and epoxy stickers from Deluxe Designs.

Friends Are Like Flowers

DESIGN BY JEANNE WYNHOFF

Form a 5½ x 4¼-inch card from light green card stock. Ink edges of card.

Cut a 5-inch piece of ribbon in half, then knot ends together. Adhere ribbon across a 5⁵⁄₁₆ x 4⅛-inch piece of printed paper 1 inch from bottom edge, with knot approximately 1¼ inches from left-hand edge, wrapping left-hand end over edge to back; tape end to reverse side of paper. (Other end of ribbon will not extend all the way across right-hand edge of card.)

Apply rub-on transfers to spell "friends are like flowers" 1 inch from fold.

Die-cut three flowers from brown card stock; die-cut flower centers from different colors within printed paper. Dot flowers with gel pen. Adhere flowers and centers to lower right quadrant of card, concealing end of ribbon.

Adhere printed paper panel to card. ■

MATERIALS

Card stock: light green, brown textured
Green/brown/pink striped printed paper
Brown ink pad
Alphabet rub-on transfers
³⁄₁₆-inch-wide brown ribbon
Die-cutting tool with flower dies
White gel pen
Transparent tape
Adhesive dots

SOURCES: Printed paper from K&Company; die-cutting tool and dies from Ellison/Sizzix.

You Are So Sweet

DESIGN BY JEANNE WYNHOFF

MATERIALS

Card stock: textured brown, textured pale pink, red, dark brown
Brown paper bag
Brown ink
2 red mini brads
¼-inch-wide tan ribbon
Die-cutting tool with ice-cream cone die
Label maker with matte black label tape
Crimper
Stapler with staples
Paper piercer *or* ¹⁄₁₆-inch hole punch
Transparent tape
Paper adhesive

Form a 4¼ x 5½-inch card from brown card stock.

Run a 3⅝ x 4-inch piece cut from the paper bag through the crimper and ink edges. Referring to photo for placement throughout, adhere crimped paper toward top of card at an angle.

Ink edges of a 2¾ x 3-inch piece of pink textured card stock; adhere to brown paper at an angle. Staple corners.

Referring to photo for colors, die-cut ice-cream cone components. Ink edges of cone; adhere components to pink card stock.

Cut a 5-inch piece of ribbon in half, then knot ends together. Adhere ribbon across bottom half of card at an angle, poking holes through card and poking ends of ribbon through holes; tape ribbon ends on reverse side of card. Set mini brads in holes at ends of ribbon.

Print "YOU ARE SO SWEET!" on label tape; peel off backing strip and adhere label tape at an angle to lower right corner of card, below ribbon. ■

SOURCES: Die-cutting tool and dies from Ellison/Sizzix; label maker and tape from DYMO Corp.

Easter Chick

DESIGN BY SUSAN HUBER

Project note: Adhere all elements using paper adhesive unless instructed otherwise.

Form a 4¼ x 5½-inch card from pale green card stock.

Die-cut or punch a 1⅜-inch circle from yellow card stock; chalk edges. Cut a small triangle from orange card stock for beak; adhere to circle. Chalk cheek areas. Dot on eyes with black marker. Adhere three tiny strips of yellow card stock to back of head for feathers.

Center and adhere chick to a 1½-inch square of lime green printed card stock using foam tape. Adhere panel to green card stock and trim, leaving a ⅛-inch border. Adhere to white card stock and trim, leaving a ¼-inch border. Center and adhere chick panel to card ⅞ inch from top.

Carefully cut a ½-inch slit through spine of card 1 inch from bottom to accommodate ribbon. Thread ribbon through slot; wrap around card front and knot ends on front, toward left edge. Mount Easter brads through ribbon and card front near right-hand edge, bending prongs *under* ribbon inside card so that they are concealed by ribbon. ∎

SOURCES: Brads from Queen & Co.; die-cutting tool and die from QuicKutz Inc.

MATERIALS

Card stock: textured pale green, textured green, textured yellow, textured orange, lime green-on-green print, white
Yellow chalk
Black fine-tip marker
3 yellow Easter brads
⅜-inch-wide yellow-and-white gingham-checked ribbon
Die-cutting tool (optional)
1⅜-inch circle die *or* punch
Paper adhesive
Adhesive foam tape

MATERIALS

Card stock: purple, green

Green-and-white gingham-
checked printed paper

Rub-on transfers: purple
and blue "Laugh with
me!," green "Sing,"
purple musical note and
streamer

2 (¹³⁄₁₆-inch) green self-
adhesive buttons

Chalks: violet, green,
shimmery lilac, shimmery
green

Die-cutting tool with 2-inch
and 3-inch flower dies

Paper adhesive

Adhesive foam squares

Sing & Laugh

DESIGNS BY TAMI MAYBERRY

Sing

Form a 6 x 4-inch top-fold card
from green card stock. Center and
adhere a 5¾ x 3¾-inch piece of purple
card stock to front of card.

Adhere a 5¾ x 1-inch strip of
printed paper across card ⁵⁄₁₆ inch from
bottom edge.

Die-cut a 3-inch flower from
green card stock and a 2-inch
flower from purple card stock.
Chalk edges of purple flower with
violet, then shimmery lilac chalk. Chalk
edges of green flower with green, then shimmery
green chalk.

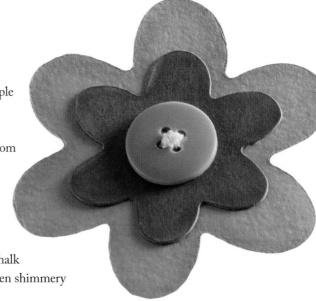

Center and adhere green self-adhesive button to purple flower; center and adhere purple
flower to green flower. Adhere flowers to left side of card using foam squares.

Apply green "sing" rub-on transfer to card as shown; apply purple musical note rub-on
transfer to border strip below flowers.

Laugh

Form a 6 x 4-inch top-fold card from purple card stock. Center and adhere a 5¾ x 3¾-inch
piece of green card stock to front of card.

Center and adhere a 5¾ x 1-inch strip of printed paper to a 5¾ x 1¼-inch strip of purple
card stock; adhere assembled strip across card ⁵⁄₁₆ inch from bottom edge.

Die-cut a 2-inch flower from purple card stock. Chalk edges with violet, then shimmery lilac
chalk. Center and adhere green self-adhesive button to flower. Adhere flower to left side of card
with adhesive foam squares.

Apply "Laugh with me!" rub-on transfer to card as shown; apply purple streamer rub-on
transfer to border strip. ■

SOURCES: Printed paper from Imagination Project Inc./Gin-X; rub-on transfers from The C-Thru Ruler Co./Déjá Views; buttons from EK Success Ltd.; die-cutting tool and dies from Ellison/Sizzix.

Flowers Say Hello

DESIGN BY SUSAN HUBER

MATERIALS

- Card stock: textured light yellow, textured yellow, yellow-orange
- Yellow-on-yellow flowers printed paper
- Flower phrase rubber stamp
- Yellow-orange dye ink
- White pearl paint
- Die-cutting tool with daisy die
- Paper adhesive
- Adhesive foam tape

Project note: *Adhere all elements using paper adhesive unless instructed otherwise.*

Form a 5½ x 4¼-inch top-fold card from light yellow card stock.

Cut a smooth, curved edge along the top of a 5½ x 3-inch piece of printed paper; adhere printed paper to front of card with bottom edges even.

Die-cut seven daisies from yellow card stock; adhere to card along curved edge of printed paper. Dot center of each daisy with white pearl paint; let dry.

Stamp flower phrase in center of a 2 x 1¾-inch piece of light yellow card stock; adhere to yellow-orange card stock and trim, leaving very narrow borders. Adhere stamped panel to upper right corner of card using foam tape. ∎

SOURCES: Printed paper from Doodlebug Design Inc.; rubber stamp from Hero Arts Rubber Stamps; paint from Ranger Industries; die-cutting tool and die from QuicKutz Inc.

Ebony & Ivory

DESIGN BY SUSAN HUBER

Project note: *Adhere all elements using paper adhesive unless instructed otherwise.*

Form a 5½ x 4¼-inch top-fold card from card stock.

Tear the upper right corner off a 5¼ x 4-inch piece of printed paper; center and adhere to front of card. Stamp musical score images on exposed black corner of card.

Adhere slide mount to lower left corner of card with foam tape. Die-cut three sets of daisy petals from card stock; assemble with mini brad through their centers. Curl petals back gently over the back of a spoon. Center and adhere daisy in slide mount opening. ■

SOURCES: Printed paper from Creative Imaginations; slide mount from Boxer Scrapbook Productions; die-cutting tool and die from QuicKutz Inc.

MATERIALS

Black card stock

Musical score printed paper

Black slide mount with
    round opening

Musical score rubber stamp

White dye ink

Matte white mini brad

Die-cutting tool with large
    daisy die

Kitchen spoon

Paper adhesive

Adhesive foam tape

Tag Thanks

DESIGN BY SUSAN HUBER

MATERIALS

Green card stock

Green striped printed paper

Green-and-white gingham-
checked ribbon

Green fibers

Die-cutting tool

Dies: ⅞ x 1⅝-inch oval tags,
¹¹⁄₁₆-inch alphabet

Paper adhesive

Adhesive foam tape

Project note: Adhere elements using paper adhesive unless instructed otherwise.

Form a 5½ x 4¼-inch top-fold card from card stock. Center and adhere a 5½ x 2½-inch piece of printed paper across front of card ⅛ inch from fold.

Die-cut six oval tags from card stock. Knot fibers through holes in tags. Center and adhere tags across printed paper on card with foam tape.

Die-cut letters to spell "thanks" from printed paper; adhere one letter to each tag.

Adhere ribbon across front of card over bottom edge of printed-paper panel. Wrap fiber around front of card just below ribbon; knot ends. ■

SOURCE: Die-cutting tool and dies from QuicKutz Inc.

Sassy Card

DESIGN BY SUSAN HUBER

Form a 4¼ x 5½-inch card from card stock.

Adhere a 1¾ x 5⅛-inch strip of white printed paper down card front ⅛ inch from right-hand edge. Cut a 3½ x 5⅛-inch piece of orange printed paper; tear off about ½ inch down right-hand side. Chalk torn edge. Attach hanger die cut to torn paper ⅞ inch from top edge with copper mini brad.

Fold a 1¼ x 4-inch strip of white printed paper in half; fringe bottom edges with scissors. "Hang" folded paper over hanger; adhere to card front.

Adhere torn paper to card overlapping white printed paper, and positioning left edge about ⅛ inch from fold.

Stamp "sassy" across bottom of towel just above fringe. Adhere shoe die cuts to lower right corner of torn printed paper panel. ■

SOURCES: Printed papers from Die Cuts With A View; die cuts from QuicKutz Inc.; stamp from Making Memories.

MATERIALS

White card stock

Polka-dot printed papers:
   oranges on orange,
   oranges on white

Die cuts: orange hanger, 2
   orange-and-white shoes

"Sassy" stamp

Orange chalk

Copper mini brad

Paper adhesive

MATERIALS

Card stock: red, white

1 x ½-inch card-stock "Adore" tag

1-inch red flower die cut

Black ink pad

2 black mini brads

Sewing machine with black thread

Corner rounder punch

Paper adhesive

Adore

DESIGN BY LINDA BEESON

Form a 5¼-inch-square top-fold card from red card stock.

Round corners on a 4¼-inch square of white card stock using corner rounder punch. Ink edges with ink pad.

Using pencil, sketch heart in center of white card-stock square. Machine-stitch around heart several times without staying on lines. Erase visible pencil lines.

Attach flower die cut and "Adore" tag to white card stock with black mini brads as shown. Center and adhere white card-stock panel to card. ■

SOURCES: Tag from Making Memories; die cut from QuicKutz Inc.

Make a Wish

DESIGN BY SUSAN STRINGFELLOW

Form a 5½-inch-square striped card from card stock.

Mark the bottom edge of the card 2½ inches from lower right corner. Cut card front in from that point to upper right corner as shown in photo.

Cut four 6-inch lengths of fibers. Punch two ⅛-inch holes near left edge of die cut, ½ inch apart. Attach candle by tying two fibers through each hole. ***Option:*** *To more firmly secure candle, adhere a piece of double-sided tape between candle and die cut.*

Slide clip over bottom edge of die cut. Center and adhere die cut to card front with foam squares, overlapping diagonal edge at lower right corner. ■

SOURCES: Card stock and die cut from My Mind's Eye; clip from Provo Craft.

MATERIALS

Reversible striped card stock

"Make a wish" die cut

Multicolored fibers

Yellow birthday candle

Orange metal clip

⅛-inch hole punch

Adhesive foam squares

Double-sided tape

  (optional)

DIMENSIONAL EMBELLISHMENTS

Fibers, page pebbles, brads, slide mounts, bottle caps, chipboard letters, polymer clay—anything goes when it comes to dimensional embellishments. Dimensional cards are best delivered by hand or in protective boxes rather than in envelopes, so they will not be crumpled or crushed.

Embossed Sailboat

DESIGN BY ALICE GOLDEN

Project note: Adhere elements using glue stick unless instructed otherwise.

Form a 3⅞ x 6⅜-inch card from dark blue card stock.

Center and attach mini brad near top edge of a 3¾ x 6¾-inch piece of printed paper; adhere printed paper to card.

Dry-emboss sailboat components onto card stocks that coordinate with printed paper; trim, leaving very narrow borders.

Adhere a 2½ x 3¾-inch piece of white card stock to dark blue card stock; trim, leaving very narrow borders. Cut light blue card stock to fit across bottom of this panel; trim top edge with decorative-edge scissors; adhere. Apply "congratulations" rub-on transfer to lower right edge.

Adhere sailboat components to panel with foam tape; draw mast with blue pen.

Punch ⅛-inch holes in upper corners of panel. Thread twine through holes; trim and knot ends of twine on front, looping over mini brad on card so that sailboat panel "hangs" from mini brad. Adhere sailboat panel to card. ■

SOURCES: Printed paper from Frances Meyer Inc.; stencil from Plaid/All Night Media; rub-on transfer from K&Company.

MATERIALS

Card stock: dark blue, light
   blue, white, red, turquoise,
   2 complementary grays
   that match printed paper
Sailboat printed paper
Blue "congratulations" rub-on
   transfer
Blue waxed linen twine
Turquoise mini brad
Blue fine-tip pen
Brass sailboat stencil
Embossing stylus
Decorative-edge scissors
⅛-inch hole punch
Glue stick
Double-sided adhesive
   foam tape

MATERIALS

Turquoise card stock

Green/blue flowers printed
paper

1⅞-inch-square green/blue
flower chipboard coaster

⁷⁄₁₆-inch-wide green/blue
polka-dot cotton tape

1¼-inch green fabric "IT'S
YOUR DAY" tag

Fine-grit sandpaper

Paper adhesive

It's Your Day

DESIGN BY SHERRY WRIGHT

Form a 6-inch-square top-fold card from card stock. Adhere a 6-inch square of printed paper to front of card.

Sand edges of coaster; adhere to card as shown in photo.

Adhere a 6-inch piece of cotton tape across card 1 inch from bottom edge. Adhere fabric tag over cotton tape ½ inch from right-hand edge. ■

SOURCES: Printed paper, coaster and cotton tape from Imagination Project Inc./Gin-X; fabric tag from Making Memories.

Falling Snow

DESIGN BY SHERRY WRIGHT

Adhere a 5½ x 4¼-inch piece of printed paper to front of card with adhesive.

Adhere "FALLING SNOW" embellishment to lower right corner with foam dots. Adhere snowflakes to card with foam dots. ■

SOURCES: Printed paper from Paper Salon; snowflakes from EK Success/Jolee's Boutique; embellishment from me & my BIG ideas.

MATERIALS

5½ x 4¼-inch light blue top-
   fold card
Snowflakes printed paper
Beaded snowflakes
"FALLING SNOW"
   embellishment
Adhesive foam dots
Paper adhesive

MATERIALS

Dark green textured
card stock

Reversible solid tan/
diamonds printed paper

Maroon fluid ink chalk

"Thinking of You Warms My
Heart" transparent sticker

Wooden snowman
embellishment

⅞-inch-wide sheer
burgundy ribbon

Die-cutting tool

Circle dies: 2-inch, 1¾-inch

Transparent tape

Paper adhesive

Adhesive foam tape

Adhesive dots

Heartwarming Greeting

DESIGN BY JEANNE WYNHOFF

Form a 4¼ x 5½-inch card from card stock.

Ink edges on the diamonds side of a 5½ x 4¼-inch piece of printed paper. Knot a 7-inch piece of ribbon 2 inches from end. Referring to photo for placement throughout, adhere to printed paper; wrap ends to reverse side and tape. Adhere printed paper to card front using adhesive.

Die-cut one 2-inch circle and one 1¾-inch circle from printed paper; turn larger circle tan side up and smaller circle diamonds side up. Ink edges. Center and adhere smaller circle to larger circle using adhesive. Adhere circles over ribbon near right-hand edge using foam tape. Adhere snowman to left-hand edge of circles using adhesive dots. Apply sticker to card in lower left corner. ∎

SOURCES: Printed paper from The C-Thru Ruler Co./Déjá Views; sticker from EK Success Ltd.; die-cutting tool and dies from Ellison/Sizzix.

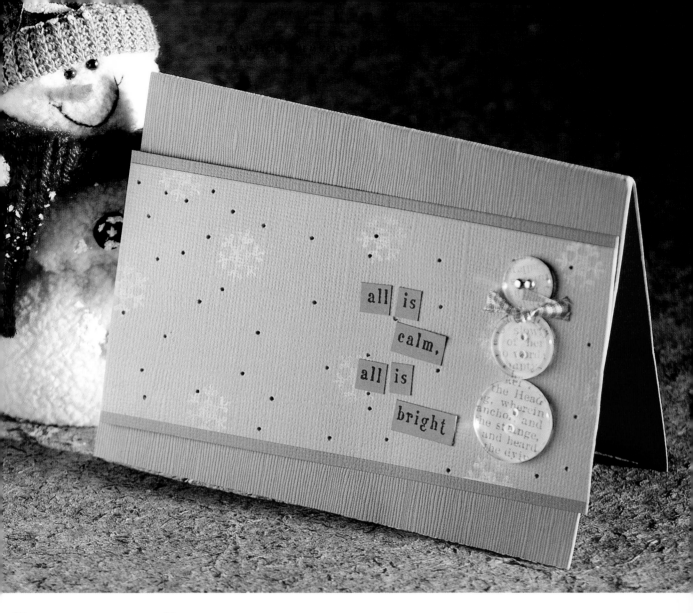

Button Snowman

DESIGN BY JENNIFER MCGUIRE

Randomly stamp a 5⅞ x 2¾-inch piece of light blue card stock with white snowflakes; pierce randomly with large needle. Center and adhere to a 5⅞ x 3-inch piece of lavender card stock; center and adhere to card.

Punch ⅞-inch, ¾-inch and 9/16-inch circles from printed paper; adhere circles to backs of matching buttons so printing is visible from front. Poke through button holes with needle. Set mini brads in holes in smallest button for eyes.

Adhere buttons to right-hand side of card, building a snowman. Cut a tiny triangle of orange card stock for nose; adhere to head. Knot a short length of ribbon; adhere at snowman's neck for scarf.

Stamp "all is calm, all is bright" in black on lavender card stock. Cut words apart; adhere to card as shown in photo. ■

SOURCES: Printed paper from Autumn Leaves; rubber stamps from Hero Arts Rubber Stamps.

MATERIALS

5⅞ x 4¼-inch blue
    card-stock card

Textured card stock: light
    blue, lavender, orange

"Printed page" printed paper

Rubber stamps: 3/16-inch
    alphabet, snowflake

Inks: white chalk, black

Transparent buttons:
    ⅞-inch, ¾-inch, 9/16-inch

2 silver mini brads

¼-inch-wide blue-and-white
    gingham-checked ribbon

Circle punches: ⅞-inch, ¾-
    inch, 9/16-inch

Large needle

Glue stick

MATERIALS

Card stock: yellow, black, white

5¾ x 4⅜-inch white envelope

Rubber stamps: daisy, "thank you," dot background, typewriter alphabet

Black ink pad

3 (½-inch) round acrylic page pebbles

¼-inch-wide black-and-white gingham-checked ribbon

Yellow colored pencil

Glue stick

Adhesive dot

Adhesive foam dots

Fresh As a Daisy

DESIGN BY SANDRA GRAHAM SMITH

Project note: Adhere elements using glue stick unless instructed otherwise.

Form a 5½ x 4¼-inch top-fold card from yellow card stock. Stamp top half of card with dot background stamp.

Randomly stamp daisy images on a 5½ x 2-inch strip of white card stock; stamp one daisy in center of a 2¼-inch square of white card stock. Color flower centers with colored pencil.

Adhere strip across card 1⅛ inches from bottom edge. Adhere strips of ribbon across card, covering top and bottom edges of white strip.

Center and adhere stamped white square to a 2½-inch square of black card stock. Adhere square panel near right edge using foam dots. Tie a small bow from ribbon; adhere to upper left corner of square panel using adhesive dot.

Stamp "thank you" across bottom of card, leaving room for "MOM" in lower right corner. Stamp "MOM" on white card stock using typewriter alphabet stamps; cut out individual letters. Adhere letters to card front; adhere page pebble over each letter.

Envelope: Stamp daisies down left edge of envelope; color flower centers with colored pencil. Adhere ribbon down stamped edge of card; trim ribbon ends even with envelope. ■

SOURCES: Rubber stamps from Hero Arts Rubber Stamps, Stampin' Up! and River City Rubber Works.

MATERIALS

5½ x 4¼-inch white top-fold
card

Card stock: white, light blue,
light green, light orange

Self-adhesive notes *or* scrap
paper

Rubber stamps: strip image,
1–1½-inch flowers,
"grateful"

Ink pads: black, light blue,
light green, light orange

Glitter

Clear glaze

¼-inch-wide black-and-white
gingham-checked ribbon

¼-inch hole punch

Mini adhesive dots

Grateful

DESIGN BY LISA JOHNSON

Mask off bottom half of card front with self-adhesive notes or scraps of paper. Ink strip image stamp with light blue, light green and light orange inks as shown; stamp top half of card, staggering images.

Stamp flowers in black over colored blocks on card *and* onto light blue, light green and light orange scraps of card stock. Punch ¼-inch circles from centers of flowers stamped on card-stock scraps; adhere over centers of flowers on card with mini adhesive dots as follows: light blue circles on light green, light green circles on light orange, light orange circle on light blue. Dot flower centers with crystal glaze; sprinkle with glitter.

Mask off bottom portion of card, leaving area exposed in lower right corner for stamping light blue strip image. Stamp "grateful" in black on top of light blue stamped strip.

Wrap ribbon around front of card; knot ends on front and trim ends. ∎

SOURCE: Card stock, rubber stamps, ink pads and glaze from Stampin' Up!

Blue Velvet Thank You

DESIGN BY SHERRY WRIGHT

MATERIALS

5½ x 4¼-inch white
   top-fold card

White card stock

Blue/brown printed papers:
   floral, polka dots

"thank you" fabric tag

¼-inch-wide light blue
   velvet trim

Paper adhesive

Adhere a 5½ x 2-inch piece of polka-dot printed paper across bottom of card. Adhere a 5½ x 3-inch piece of floral printed paper across top of card.

Adhere a 6½-inch piece of velvet trim over seam between printed papers; wrap ends over edges of card and adhere to reverse side. Adhere a 5⅜ x 4-inch piece of card stock to reverse side of card front, concealing ends of velvet trim.

Adhere "thank you" fabric tag to front of card 1 inch from top and 1¼ inches from left-hand edge. ■

SOURCES: Printed papers from Chatterbox; "thank you" tag from Making Memories.

Grateful Greetings

DESIGN BY STACEY STAMITOLES

MATERIALS

5½ x 4¼-inch red
   card-stock card

Red card stock

Printed papers: black-and-
   white grid, gray-on-white
   polka dots

Acrylic "thanks" charm

½-inch-wide black-and-
   white daisy trim

1¾-inch circle punch

Adhesive dots

Tear 1 inch off bottom edge of card's front flap. Adhere a 5½ x ¾-inch piece of polka-dot printed paper to front flap behind torn edge, leaving ¾ inch of card's back flap exposed across bottom. Adhere daisy trim to back flap across exposed edge.

Tear ½ inch off the bottom edge of a 5¼ x 3½-inch piece of grid printed paper; center and adhere paper to red portion of card flap. Adhere a 5¼ x ⅝-inch strip of polka-dot printed paper to card 1 inch from fold.

Punch a 1¾-inch circle from red card stock; center over polka-dot paper strip and adhere to card ⅝ inch from left-hand edge. Center and adhere acrylic charm to circle. ∎

SOURCES: Printed papers from Scrapworks and Junkitz; acrylic charm from Go West Studios.

Thanks

DESIGN BY TAMI MAYBERRY

Form a 7 x 5-inch top-fold card from red card stock. Round corners of a 6 x 4½-inch piece of printed paper using corner rounder punch; adhere paper to card.

Cut a 2½ x 5-inch piece of light yellow card stock; tear along right-hand edge and adhere to left-hand edge of card, edges even. Cut a 1½ x 5-inch piece of red card stock; tear along right-hand edge and adhere to light yellow card stock ¼ inch from edge of card.

Adhere a 5-inch strip of ribbon to torn red card-stock strip ½ inch from left-hand edge; glue metal flowers, evenly spaced, down ribbon using gem glue.

Attach mini brad to metal "thank you" tag; glue tag to lower right corner of card using gem glue. ∎

SOURCES: Printed paper from Sweetwater; metal flowers from Making Memories; metal "thank you" tag from K&Company.

MATERIALS

Card stock: red, light yellow

Red-and-yellow flowers printed paper

3 metal flowers

Metal oval "thank you" tag

Mini brad

¼-inch-wide sheer red ribbon

Paper adhesive

Gem glue

Best of the Bunch

MATERIALS

4½ x 6¼-inch textured yellow card

Card stock: white, orange, black linen

Stickers: 3-D spring flowers, transparent "you are special"

¼-inch-wide black-and-white striped ribbon

Paper punches: 1¼ x ⁹⁄₁₆-inch tag, ⅛-inch hole

Glue stick

Adhesive foam tape

DESIGN BY SANDI GENOVESE, COURTESY OF MRS. GROSSMAN'S PAPER CO.

Project note: *Adhere elements using glue stick unless instructed otherwise.*

Center and adhere a 3¼ x 4⅜-inch piece of orange card stock to card ⅞ inch from top edge. Center and adhere a 3 x 4⅛-inch piece of black card stock to orange card stock with foam tape.

Punch tag from white card stock; adhere "you are special" sticker to tag. Punch ⅛-inch hole in tag; thread stem of pink tulip sticker through hole; set aside.

Build flower bouquet on sticker backing sheet: Place purple iris in center, tulip with tag on left and orange poppy on right. Position yellow daffodil on top.

Wrap ¾-inch piece of ribbon around flower stems. Peel bouquet off backing sheet; adhere to black panel on card. Tuck leaves into bouquet directly against card. ■

SOURCES: Card, stickers and ribbon from Mrs. Grossman's Paper Co.; tag punch from Uchida of America.

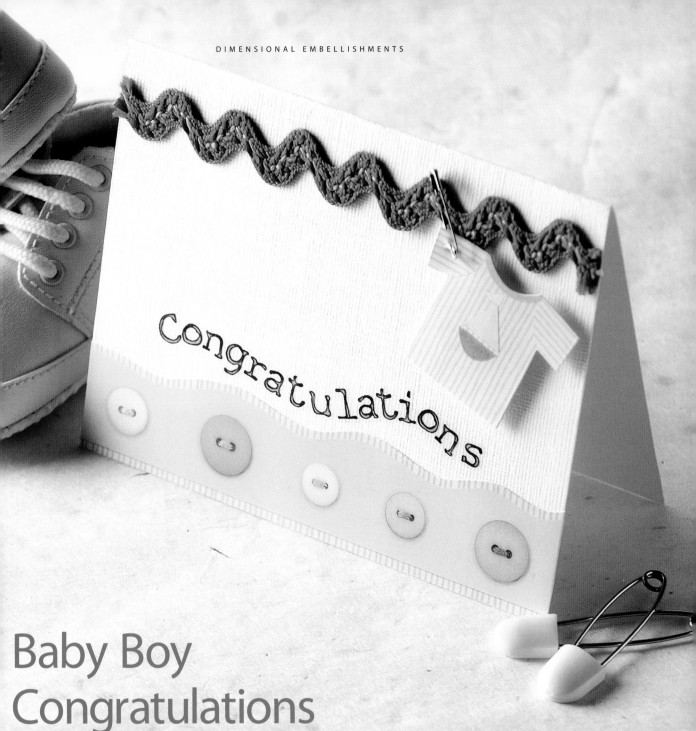

Baby Boy Congratulations

DESIGN BY DAWN MOORE

Project note: Adhere elements with paper adhesive unless instructed otherwise.

Form a 5½ x 4-inch top-fold card from card stock.

Adhere a 5½-inch piece of border sticker across bottom edge of card. Adhere "congratulations" sticker to card just above border sticker.

Adhere a 5½-inch piece of rickrack across card, ¼ inch from top fold. Poke safety pin through left sleeve of shirt sticker; adhere foam dots to back of shirt. Referring to photo for placement, adhere shirt sticker to card at an angle, near rickrack in upper right corner; poke safety pin through rickrack and close. ∎

SOURCE: Stickers from Doodlebug Design Inc. and Provo Craft.

MATERIALS

Pale yellow textured
  card stock
Stickers: baby boy
  border, baby boy
  shirt, transparent
  "Congratulations"
Multicolored blue rickrack
Small silver safety pin
Paper adhesive
Adhesive foam dots

Happy Birthday, Dad!

DESIGN BY SUSAN COBB, COURTESY OF HOT OFF THE PRESS

MATERIALS

5 x 6½-inch card

Tools-themed scrapbook
  page kit

Alphabet/word rubber
  stamps, stickers or rub-on
  transfers (optional)

Black ink pad

Paper adhesive

Adhesive foam squares

Computer with printer
  (optional)

Project note: *Adhere elements with paper adhesive unless instructed otherwise.*

Adhere a 5 x 6½-inch piece of printed paper from scrapbook page kit to front of card.

Adhere alphabet tiles to spell "DAD" down left side of card using foam squares. Referring to photo for placement throughout, adhere large tag to card using foam squares; adhere tools to tag. Tie knot in the center of a 3-inch piece of brown cord; adhere to star on tag.

Use computer to generate, or hand-print, "Happy Birthday!" on extra printed paper; trim strip around words, ink edges, and adhere near bottom of card. Use computer to generate, or hand-print, "Enjoy your day!" on extra printed paper; trim to 2½ x 3 inches and adhere inside card.

Option: *Add words with rubber stamps, stickers or rub-on transfers.*

Adhere star to upper edge using foam square. ■

SOURCE: Scrapbook page kit from Hot Off The Press.

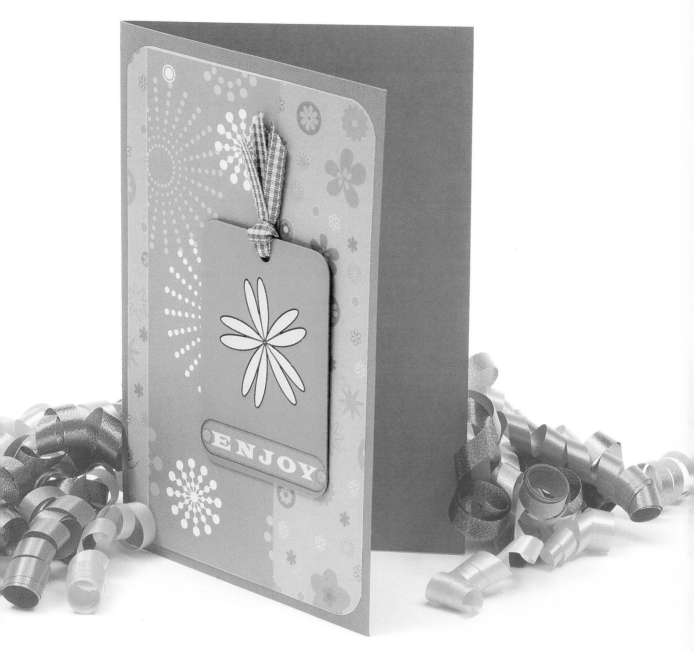

Enjoy!

DESIGN BY TAMI MAYBERRY

Form a 4 x 6-inch card from card stock.

Round corners on a 3¾ x 5¾-inch piece of blue printed paper using a corner rounder punch. Center and adhere paper to card. Adhere a 2 x 5¾-inch strip of orange printed paper to blue printed paper ½ inch from fold.

Apply flower and "ENJOY" rub-on transfers to laminate chip. Thread ribbons through hole in chip; adhere chip to card. ∎

SOURCE: Printed papers and rub-on transfers from Autumn Leaves.

MATERIALS

Orange card stock

Printed papers: orange-and-white, blue-on-blue

Rub-on transfers: white daisy, "ENJOY"

2 x 2¾-inch orange laminate chip

¼-inch-wide gingham-checked ribbon: blue-and-white, orange-and-white

Corner rounder punch

Paper adhesive

Harlequin Dreams

DESIGN BY JEANNE WYNHOFF

MATERIALS

Burgundy card stock

Diamonds printed paper

"dream" rub-on transfer

Metal flower charm

⅜-inch-wide burgundy/tan ribbon

Transparent tape

Paper adhesive

Adhesive dots

Form a 4¼ x 5½-inch card from card stock.

Adhere a 5-inch piece of ribbon across a 4⅛ x 5¼-inch piece of printed paper 1¼ inches from bottom edge; wrap ends to reverse side and tape.

Knot ends of a 5-inch and a 3-inch piece of ribbon together and adhere to printed paper at an angle, crossing first ribbon and positioning knot near right-hand edge; wrap ends to reverse side and tape.

Adhere flower charm to ribbon in lower right corner using adhesive dots. Apply "dream" rub-on transfer to right-hand side of printed paper ½ inch above ribbon. Adhere printed paper panel to card. ■

SOURCES: Printed paper from Scenic Route Paper Co.; rub-on transfer and metal charm from Making Memories.

Daydream

DESIGN BY TAMI MAYBERRY

Form a 6 x 4-inch top-fold card from blue card stock. Center and adhere a 5¾ x 3¾-inch piece of light blue card stock to card front.

Center and adhere a 5¼ x 3¼-inch piece of printed paper to a 5½ x 3½-inch piece of blue card stock. Center and set eyelets in opposite ends of paper/card-stock panel as shown in photo.

Apply "daydream" rub-on transfer to acrylic oval tag. Thread fiber through holes in tag and through eyelets; adhere fiber ends on reverse side of panel. Center and adhere panel to card. Apply orange flower rub-on transfer to one of the light blue circles in lower right corner of card. ■

SOURCES: Printed paper and rub-on transfers from Autumn Leaves; acrylic oval from Heidi Grace Designs Inc.

MATERIALS

Card stock: blue, light blue

Circles printed paper

Rub-on transfers:
   "daydream," small orange
   flower

2⅛ x 1⅛-inch acrylic oval tag

2 blue eyelets

Blue fibers

Eyelet-setting tool

Paper adhesive

MATERIALS

Card stock: light green, olive
    green, orange with green
    polka dots

Transparent
    "Congratulations" sticker

⅜-inch-wide green
    grosgrain ribbon

2 (2-inch) beaded green
    iron-on flowers

Paper adhesive

Beaded Flower Congratulations

DESIGN BY TAMI MAYBERRY

Form a 7 x 5-inch top-fold card from orange polka-dot card stock.

Adhere a 7 x 2¼-inch piece of olive green card stock to card 1¼ inches from fold. Adhere a 7 x 2-inch piece of light green card stock to olive green strip with bottom edges even. Adhere a 7-inch piece of ribbon next to bottom edge of card-stock strips.

Center and apply "Congratulations" sticker to card-stock strip. Adhere iron-on flowers with adhesive. ■

SOURCES: Printed card stock from My Mind's Eye; sticker from K&Company; iron-on flowers from Hirschberg Schutz & Co. Inc.

It's in the Bag

DESIGN BY SANDI GENOVESE, COURTESY OF MRS. GROSSMAN'S PAPER CO.

Project note: Adhere elements using glue stick unless instructed otherwise.

Center and adhere a 2½-inch square of pink card stock to card ⅞ inch from top edge. Center and adhere a 2-inch square of pearlescent light pink card stock to pink square. Adhere purse sticker over squares at an angle.

Punch tag from pearlescent light pink card stock; adhere tag to pink card stock; trim edges with decorative-edge scissors. Adhere "you are special" sticker to tag. Punch a ⅛-inch hole in end of tag; thread a 2-inch piece of ribbon through hole. Adhere tag to purse handle as shown with foam tape.

Adhere a ⅝-inch-wide strip of pink card stock across card ¾ inch from bottom edge. Center and adhere ribbon across pink card-stock strip; trim ends even with edges of card. Tie bow from another piece of ribbon; glue to ribbon on card near right-hand edge. ■

SOURCES: Card, stickers and ribbon from Mrs. Grossman's Paper Co.; card stock from Paper Garden and Paper Zone; tag punch from Uchida of America.

MATERIALS

4½ x 6¼-inch black card

Card stock: pink, pearlescent light pink

Stickers: 3-D purse, transparent "you are special"

¼-inch-wide black-and-white pin-dot ribbon

Paper punches: 1¼ x 9/16-inch tag, ⅛-inch hole

Decorative-edge scissors

Glue stick

Adhesive foam tape

Weathered Stars

DESIGN BY SUSAN HUBER

MATERIALS

White card stock

"Crackled paint" printed
paper: white over blue,
slate over blue

"Free" die cut

½-inch-wide red twill tape

Silver stars fringed trim

Paper adhesive

Adhesive foam tape

Project note: *Adhere elements using paper adhesive unless instructed otherwise.*

Form a 4¼ x 5½-inch card from card stock.

Adhere a 4¼ x 1¼-inch strip of white printed paper across top of card, top edges even.

Adhere a 4¼-inch square of slate printed paper across bottom of card, bottom edges even.

Adhere silver star fringed trim over seam between card stocks; adhere twill tape over edge of fringed trim.

Adhere "free" die cut to lower right corner of card with foam tape. ■

SOURCES: Printed paper from EK Success Ltd.; die cut from O'Scrap; twill tape from Fibers By The Yard.

Asian Influence

DESIGN BY SUSAN HUBER

MATERIALS

Red card stock

Red-and-white printed
papers: floral, gauze
weave

"Adore" stamp

Black dye ink

Red paper mini umbrella

Red fiber and ribbon

2 red mini brads

Vintage-style brad

Paper adhesive

Adhesive foam tape

Project note: Adhere elements using paper adhesive unless instructed otherwise.

Form a 5½ x 4¼-inch top-fold card from card stock.

Cut a 5¼ x 4-inch piece from both printed papers. Tear off upper right corner of floral piece at an angle, leaving torn edge; adhere to gauze-weave paper with side and bottom edges even.

Wrap ribbon and fibers vertically around printed papers 1 inch from left edge; tie ends on front. Snap "pole" off umbrella; flatten umbrella and adhere to printed papers near top. Attach vintage-style brad through umbrella center.

Stamp "Adore" onto gauze-weave printed paper; cut out word centered in a 1½ x ¾-inch rectangle. Adhere rectangle to card stock and trim, leaving a narrow border. Affix mini brads through ends of rectangle and position near bottom of printed papers, overlapping umbrella edge; adhere with foam tape.

Center and adhere panel to card. ■

SOURCES: Printed papers from Die Cuts With A View; rubber stamp and vintage brad from Making Memories.

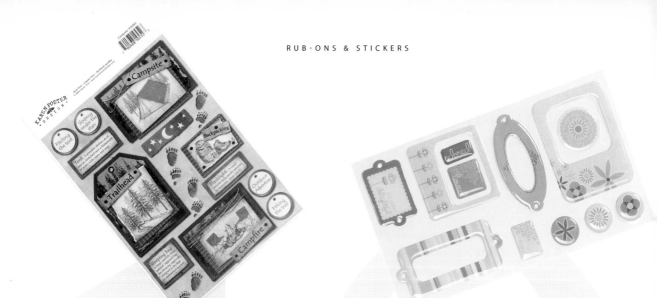

RUB-ONS & STICKERS

From sentiments to borders to graphic elements, rub-on transfers and stickers cover it all. Among the most versatile of embellishments, rub-ons and stickers are easy to use and fun to collect and trade with your friends.

Stamped With Love

DESIGN BY REBECCA COOPER

Cut four stickers spelling "LOVE" in one piece from sticker sheet. Adhere stickers to a 4⅛ x 9⅛-inch piece of card stock 1⅜ inches from top.

Using white thread, machine-stitch around stickers ¼ inch from sticker edges. ■

SOURCE: Stickers from Karen Foster Design.

MATERIALS
Light green card stock
Alphabet postage-stamp
   sticker sheet
Sewing machine with white
   thread
Paper adhesive

Pet Lover Greetings

MATERIALS

Green card stock

Dog-themed printed paper:
rust, light green

Cat-themed printed paper:
tan with stripes, light tan

Transparent dog- and cat-
themed stickers

Paper adhesive

DESIGNS BY SHERRY WRIGHT

Dog Card

Form a 6-inch-square top-fold card from card stock. Adhere rust printed paper to card leaving very narrow green margins at top and bottom. Adhere a 6 x 2-inch strip of green printed paper to card ½ inch from bottom.

Referring to photo for placement, adhere paw print, dog bone and quotation stickers to card.

Cat Card

Form a 5 x 6-inch top-fold card from card stock. Adhere tan striped printed paper to card. Adhere a 5 x 2¼-inch strip of light tan printed paper to card ¼ inch from bottom.

Referring to photo for placement, adhere "meow" and quotation stickers to card. ■

SOURCE: Printed papers and stickers from Autumn Leaves.

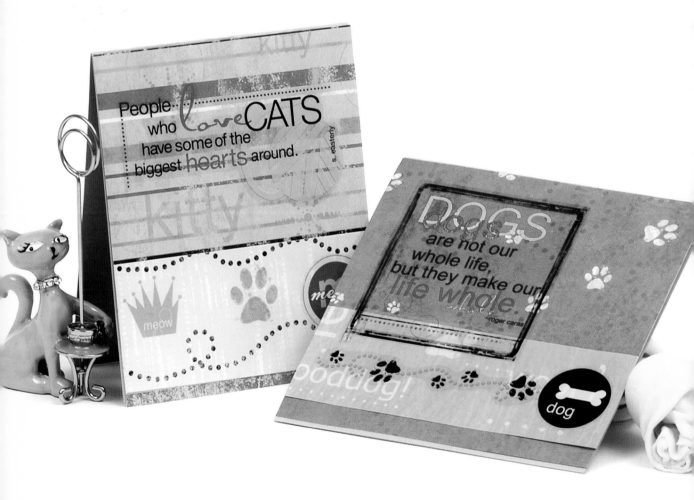

Be Happy

DESIGN BY JEANNE WYNHOFF

Form a 4¼ x 5½-inch card from card stock. Adhere a 4¼ x 5½-inch piece of printed paper to card front.

Adhere a 4¼ x 1-inch card-stock border sticker across card 1⅛ inches inch from top. Adhere "happiness is" quotation sticker over border sticker ⅜ inch from fold.

Referring to photo for placement throughout, adhere a 2⅝ x ⅜-inch strip of flower border sticker to right side of card and a flower card-stock sticker over border sticker. Trim "be happy" from card-stock sticker; adhere to card, overlapping lower left corner of flower sticker. ∎

SOURCE: Printed paper and card-stock stickers from Carolee's Creations & Co.

MATERIALS

Blue card stock

Blue/black dots printed paper

Blue/white card-stock stickers: border, flower, "be happy," "happiness is" quotation

Paper adhesive

MATERIALS

4¼ x 5½-inch white card

Multicolor circles printed
  paper

1¼-inch round blue "THANK
  YOU" sticker

⅞-inch-wide blue/yellow
  striped ribbon

Paper adhesive

Graphic Thank You

DESIGN BY SHERRY WRIGHT

Adhere ribbon across a 4¼ x 5½-inch piece of printed paper 1¼ inches from bottom, wrapping ribbon ends over edges and adhering to reverse side. Adhere printed paper to card front.

Referring to photo for placement, adhere "thank you" sticker over ribbon. ■

SOURCES: Printed paper from Scenic Route Paper Co.; sticker from Die Cuts With A View; ribbon from Offray.

Fall Frolic

DESIGN BY DAWN MOORE

Form a 4¼ x 5½-inch card from card stock.

Adhere a 4 x ¼-inch strip of printed paper to card near top. Referring to photo throughout for placement, adhere card-stock stickers along fold and across bottom of card, leaving even borders and margins.

Apply "Fall" rub-on transfer to printed paper. Punch a 1-inch circle from printed paper, centering rub-on transfer in circle. Ink edges using brown chalk ink and adhere circle to metal-rimmed tag.

Attach a 1½-inch piece of ribbon to top of tag using mini brad. Adhere tag to lower right corner of card. Adhere leaf to card. ∎

SOURCES: Printed paper from Scenic Route Paper Co.; card-stock stickers from Imagination Project/Gin-X; rub-on transfers from Chatterbox; ribbon from May Arts.

MATERIALS

Rust card stock

Striped printed paper in fall
colors

Fall-themed card-stock
stickers

1¼-inch round metal-
rimmed tag

Brown chalk ink

Black "Fall" rub-on transfer

Silver mini brad

Orange silk leaf

¼-inch-wide tan-and-brown
gingham-checked ribbon

1-inch circle punch

Paper adhesive

Give the Magic of the Season

DESIGN BY SHERRY WRIGHT

MATERIALS

Reversible gold leaves
   printed card stock
Transparent "Give the magic
   of the season" sticker
Brown distress ink
Gold-on-gold jacquard
   fabric accents: pinked ⅞-
   inch-wide strip, 3¼-inch-
   square frame
Brown fringed fiber
Paper adhesive

Form a 5 x 6-inch top-fold card from printed card stock with gold/crackle side on outside. Ink edges using distress ink.

Adhere sticker to reverse side of a 2½-inch square cut from printed card stock. Adhere card-stock/sticker panel 1 inch from upper left corner.

Wrap fiber around bottom of fabric frame and adhere to card over sticker. Adhere fabric strip to card ½ inch from bottom. ■

SOURCES: Printed card stock from PrintWorks; sticker from Autumn Leaves; fabric accents from EK Success Ltd.

Autumn Greetings

DESIGN BY ALICE GOLDEN

Cut printed paper slightly smaller than card front and adhere to card.

Adhere sticker to a 3⅛ x 2¾-inch piece of card stock. Color image using watercolor pencils; blend colors with watercolor brush and water.

Apply copper tape over top and bottom edges of card stock and adhere to card ¾ inch from top. ■

SOURCES: Printed paper from Frances Meyer Inc.; sticker from Stampendous!; copper tape from Karen Foster Design.

MATERIALS

- 4¼ x 5⅝-inch ivory card
- Natural card stock
- Wheat printed paper
- Copper "thinking of you" sticker
- Watercolor pencils: orange, brown, terra-cotta, gold, green
- Watercolor brush
- Copper tape
- Paper adhesive

Scarecrows, corn rows
pumpkins on the vine
leaves curl, wind swirls
fall is right on time

All About Autumn

DESIGNS BY JEANNE WYNHOFF

Large Card

Form a 5½ x 8½-inch card from brown card stock.

Adhere large scarecrow sticker to orange card stock and trim, leaving a narrow border; adhere to brown card stock and trim, leaving a narrow border. Adhere the scarecrows poem sticker to orange card stock and trim.

Referring to photo throughout for placement, adhere a 3-inch piece of ribbon to a 5¼ x 8¼-inch piece of printed paper, wrapping right-hand end of ribbon over edge and adhering it to reverse side.

Adhere scarecrow panel over ribbon end. Adhere scarecrow poem overlapping upper right edge of scarecrow. Adhere embellished printed paper panel to card.

Knot ribbon through holes in button. Trim ribbon ends and adhere button to ribbon on card using foam square.

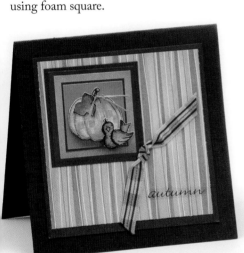

Small Cards

For each card, form a 4¾-inch-square card from dark brown card stock.

Referring to photo throughout, embellish a 3¾ x 3⅝-inch piece of striped printed paper as desired using ribbon, staples, transparent sticker or rub-on transfer, and a 2-inch card-stock sticker adhered to a 2¼-inch square of the second dark brown card stock. If desired, adhere matted sticker to layout using foam squares for added dimension.

Adhere layout to a 4-inch square of second dark brown card stock and adhere to card front. ■

MATERIALS

Textured card stock: brown, orange, 2 dark browns with different textures

Striped printed paper in fall colors

Card-stock stickers: 3³⁄₁₆ x 6⅝-inch scarecrow with corn shock, 2¾ x 1¾-inch scarecrows poem, 2-inch-square sunflowers and pumpkins

Transparent autumn sentiment stickers

Autumn sentiment rub-on transfers

⅞-inch flat orange button

⅜-inch-wide orange/black/red striped ribbon

Stapler with staples

Double-sided tape

Adhesive foam squares

SOURCES: Printed paper from Frances Meyer Inc.; card-stock stickers from Bo-Bunny Press; transparent stickers from EK Success Ltd.; ribbon from Fibers By The Yard.

Santa's On His Way

DESIGN BY JEANNE WYNHOFF

MATERIALS

Green card stock

"Stitched" red-and-cream
striped printed paper

Card-stock stickers: Santa in
sleigh, gift boxes

Fibers: red, cream

Metal gift-box charm

Paper adhesive

Adhesive dots

Form a 4¼ x 5½-inch card from card stock.

Knot two pieces of fiber together; adhere to a 4¼ x 5½-inch piece of printed paper 1 inch from bottom with knot 1¼ inches from right edge. Wrap fiber ends over edges and adhere to reverse side. Adhere printed paper to card.

Referring to photo for placement throughout, adhere Santa sticker and three gift-box stickers to a 3½ x 4-inch piece of green card stock. Adhere card stock to card ⅛ inch from top.

Adhere metal gift-box charm to printed paper over knot using adhesive dots. ■

SOURCES: Printed paper from Sweetwater; card-stock stickers from Karen Foster Design; fibers from Fibers By The Yard; charm from JoAnn's.

Winter Wonderland

DESIGN BY SHERRY WRIGHT

Form a 5 x 6-inch top-fold card from yellow card stock. Cut a piece of checked printed paper to fit card front; adhere a 9/16-inch-wide strip of striped printed paper to checked printed paper rectangle 3/8 inch from left edge.

Adhere printed twill tape 1/2 inch from bottom edge of paper rectangle, wrapping ends of tape over edges and adhering on reverse side. Knot ribbon through hole in top of card stock tag and adhere tag to rectangle. Adhere assembled panel to card front. ■

SOURCES: Printed paper from Chatterbox; card-stock tag from Deluxe Designs; ribbon from Fibers By The Yard; twill tape from Carolee's Creations & Co.

MATERIALS

Textured yellow card stock

Printed paper: blue/gray checks, blue/white stripes

2½ x 4⅞-inch snowman card-stock tag sticker

⅜-inch-wide reversible blue/ silver ribbon

1-inch-wide winter-themed printed twill tape

Paper adhesive

MATERIALS

5½ x 4¼-inch top-fold off-
white card

Card stock: off-white, pink
or blue

Printed paper: yellow/white,
baby-themed pink *or* blue

5¾ x 4⅜-inch envelope

Baby-themed 3-D card-stock
stickers

Rub-on transfers: "Special
Delivery," "girl" *or* "boy"

⁷⁄₁₆-inch-wide pink *or* blue
sheer ribbon

⅛-inch hole punch

Adhesive

Adhesive foam tape *or*
mounting squares

Special Delivery

DESIGNS BY KAREN DESMET, *COURTESY OF ANNA GRIFFIN INC.*

Cover card with yellow/white printed paper. Referring to photo for placement throughout, adhere a 2⅝ x 4¼-inch piece of off-white card stock to right-hand side of card. Adhere a 2½ x 4¼-inch piece of pink or blue printed paper to off-white card stock.

Apply "girl" or "boy" rub-on transfer to pink or blue card stock; trim around word. Cut two small tags from yellow/white printed paper; punch holes in ends. Adhere tags to pink or blue card stock; trim, leaving narrow borders. Adhere card stock with rub-on transfer to one tag; adhere over other tag as shown in photo.

Thread ribbon through holes in tags; knot. Adhere tags to card with foam tape. Adhere 3-D sticker to lower right corner.

Apply "Special Delivery" rub-on transfer to a 2 x 2½-inch piece of pink or blue card stock; adhere to reverse side of frame sticker. Adhere sticker to left side of card.

Envelope: Embellish envelope as desired with printed paper and 3-D stickers. ∎

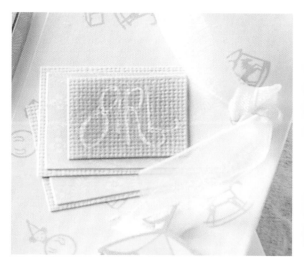

SOURCES: Printed paper and stickers from Anna Griffin Inc.; "boy" and "girl" rub-on transfers from Making Memories.

MATERIALS

White card stock

Printed papers: orange/
    brown/green stripes,
    green brushstrokes

Halloween-themed card-
    stock stickers

2 orange mini brads

Paper piercer *or* large needle

Paper adhesive

Halloween Hello

DESIGN BY SHERRY WRIGHT

Form a 4¼ x 5½-inch card from card stock. Adhere striped printed paper to front.

Referring to photo for placement throughout, adhere a 3-inch square of green brushstrokes printed paper.

Cut "Halloween" label from stickers; punch holes in ends and attach mini brads in holes. Adhere sticker to card. Adhere vintage jack-o'-lantern sticker over lower right corner of green square. Cut bats from Halloween stickers and adhere to card. ∎

SOURCES: Printed paper from Rusty Pickle; stickers from Crafty Secrets Publications.

Red Flower Celebration

DESIGN BY LINDA BEESON

MATERIALS

White textured card stock

Circles printed paper

Blue chalk ink pad

Red rub-on transfers:
    "celebrate," flowers

Paper adhesive

Form a 5-inch-square card from card stock; ink edges. Position fold on left.

Adhere a 3-inch circle motif cut from the printed paper to lower right corner. Referring to photo for placement, apply "celebrate" and red flower rub-on transfers to circle. ∎

SOURCES: Printed paper from American Crafts; ink pad from Clearsnap Inc.; rub-on transfers from KI Memories.

Framed Love

DESIGN BY KATHLEEN PANEITZ

White card stock

Pink/brown printed paper

1⅜-inch "february" card-
stock tag

3 x 2⅝-inch flat white slide-
mount–style wooden
frame

Date stamp

Sepia ink

¾-inch-square pink/brown
woven alphabet labels to
spell "love"

Pink "Happy Valentine's Day"
rub-on transfer

Pink mini safety pin

⅝-inch-wide brown-on-
pink polka-dot grosgrain
ribbon

Fine sandpaper

Permanent adhesive

Form a 4¾ x 4-inch top-fold card from card stock. Adhere printed paper to card front and sand edges lightly. Referring to photo throughout for placement, adhere woven alphabet labels in a block to spell "love."

Ink edges of wooden frame using sepia ink. Tie ribbon around left side of frame and trim ends. Adhere frame to card to frame "love."

Apply "Happy Valentine's Day" rub-on transfer across top of frame. Attach "february" tag to ribbon using safety pin. Stamp year onto lower right corner of frame using sepia ink. ■

SOURCES: Printed paper from American Crafts; tag, rub-on transfers and woven labels from Making Memories; frame from Chatterbox; ribbon from May Arts; permanent adhesive from Beacon.

Spring Fever

DESIGN BY DAWN MOORE

Form a 5½ x 4¼-inch top-fold card from light blue card stock. Tear about ½ inch from one long edge of a 5½ x 2¼-inch strip of brown card stock. Adhere strip to card, bottom edges even.

Apply "spring fever" and "grow" rub-on transfers as shown in photo.

Adhere dark brown ribbon across top of card; trim ends even with card and apply rub-on transfers to ribbon.

Adhere printed paper to slide mount and ink edges using brown ink. Tie tan-and-brown ribbon around bottom of slide mount. Adhere slide mount to card, framing the "grow" rub-on transfer. ∎

SOURCES: Printed paper from SEI; rub-on transfers from Making Memories; ribbons from May Arts.

MATERIALS

Card stock: dark brown, textured light blue
Blue/brown daisy printed paper
Slide mount
Brown fluid chalk ink
White spring-themed rub-on transfers
Ribbon: ⅜-inch-wide brown grosgrain, ¼-inch-wide tan-and-brown gingham check
Paper adhesive

STAMPING

Rubber stamps come in all shapes and sizes, from tiny alphabet stamps to background textures that cover large areas. Stamps can be mounted on wood, foam or acrylic blocks, or can be unmounted. Stamped designs can be as simple or as elaborate as your time and imagination allow.

Love Grows

DESIGN BY LISA JOHNSON

Position card with fold at top. Ink edges and surface using green ink. Stamp "love grows …" in lower right corner using dark pink ink.

Apply dark pink ink to heart stamp and stamp on scrap paper to remove some of the ink.

Immediately roll only the edges of heart in dark pink ink, huff onto stamp to moisten ink on remainder of heart, and stamp onto a 1⅞ x 2¾-inch piece of white card stock. Stamp sprout below heart and stamp random splatter pattern using light green ink.

Paint center of heart with glue; sprinkle with glitter and tap off excess. Distress edges of card stock, rolling opposite corners.

Ink surface and edges of a 2¹¹⁄₁₆ x 3¹⁄₁₆-inch piece of dark pink card stock using dark pink ink. Punch three ¹⁄₁₆-inch holes in a vertical row in lower left corner. Mount mini brads in holes.

Adhere stamped card stock to dark pink card stock and assembled panel to card front as shown in photo. ■

SOURCE: Card and stamps from A Muse Artstamps.

MATERIALS

4¼-inch-square green card

Card stock: dark pink, white

Rubber stamps: ½-inch heart, 1¼-inch sprout, ¼-inch "love grows … ," splatter background

Inks: green, light green, dark pink

3 aged copper mini brads

Ultrafine crystal glitter

¹⁄₁₆-inch hole punch

Small brush

Clear-drying glue

Tiny adhesive dots

Olive You

DESIGN BY STACEY STAMITOLES

5½ x 4¼-inch pink top-fold
card

White card stock

Pink/brown/blue/white
paisley printed paper

Brown card-stock sticker
with white faux stitching

7⁄16-inch paper flowers: pink,
olive green

"olive you" rubber stamp

Ink pads: black, brown

Pink marker

Transparent pink seed
beads

Paper adhesive

Cut printed paper slightly smaller than card front and adhere to card. Referring to photo for placement throughout, adhere a 5½ x ⅞-inch strip of stitched card stock to card so that stitching is visible at both ends.

Stamp "olive you" image slightly left of center on a 3¾ x 1¼-inch strip of white card stock using black ink. Color heart using a pink marker. Ink edges of strip with brown ink pad and adhere strip to card at an angle.

Adhere paper flowers to ends of strip. Adhere a bead to the center of each flower. ■

SOURCE: Printed paper, card-stock sticker and rubber stamp from Paper Salon.

Typing Love Letters

DESIGN BY SANDRA GRAHAM SMITH

Form a 4¼ x 5½-inch card from red card stock.

Stamp newsprint background onto a 3¾ x 5-inch piece of pink card stock using black ink.

Stamp hearts randomly on a 2¾ x 3¾-inch piece of red card stock using watermark ink. Adhere to a 3 x 4-inch piece of black card stock. Adhere black/red panel to stamped pink card stock.

Wrap ribbon around upper left and lower right corners of pink/red/black panel; adhere ends on reverse side. Tie ribbon in a small bow; adhere to ribbon in upper left corner. Adhere panel to card.

Stamp typewriter onto white card stock using black ink. Trim around image, leaving a narrow white border. Trim out top of typewriter roller where "paper" will be positioned.

For typed page, stamp "Love" definition onto white copier paper using black ink. Cut out, trimming around tops of letters as shown, and crimp definition portion a couple of times. Adhere typewriter and typed page to red card stock panel. ∎

SOURCES: Rubber stamp from Stamp Camp, Lost Coast Designs, Posh Limited and Stamps by Judith; watermark ink from Tsukineko Inc.

MATERIALS

Card stock: red, pink, black, white

White copier paper

Rubber stamps: typewriter, "Love" definition, newsprint background, ½-inch heart

Ink pads: black, watermark

¼-inch-wide black-and-white gingham-checked ribbon

Double-sided tape

God Bless America

DESIGN BY ALICE GOLDEN

MATERIALS

5½ x 4-inch white card

Card stock: red, glossy white

Blue corrugated paper

4½ x 3¼-inch America
  collage rubber stamp

Dark blue dye ink

⁷⁄₁₆-inch-wide red, white and
  blue striped ribbon

¼-inch hole punch

Paper adhesive

Stamp collage image onto a 4¾ x 3⅜-inch piece of glossy white card stock. Adhere stamped image to red card stock; trim, leaving very narrow borders. Punch two ¼-inch holes in upper right corner; knot ribbon through holes and trim ends.

Adhere a 5⁵⁄₁₆ x 3¹³⁄₁₆-inch piece of corrugated paper to front of card with channels running horizontally. Adhere stamped panel to corrugated paper. ∎

SOURCES: rubber stamp from Impression Obsession Inc.

Light Up the Holidays

DESIGN BY KATHLEEN PANEITZ

Stamp snowman onto card. Color holly leaves and hat using watercolor pencils. Apply "happy HOLIDAYS" rub-on transfer below snowman.

Adhere jewel to hat for holly berry using glue. Adhere mini tree lights string across snowman, affixing an adhesive dot under each light bulb. ■

SOURCES: Rubber stamp from Penny Black Inc.; rub-on transfer from Making Memories.

MATERIALS

4¼ x 5½-inch ivory card

1¾ x 2-inch snowman
    rubber stamp

Black dye ink pad

"happy HOLIDAYS" rub-on
    transfer

⅛-inch red jewel

String of mini tree lights

Watercolor pencils

Clear-drying glue

Tiny adhesive dots

Polka-Dot Christmas

DESIGN BY SUSAN HUBER

MATERIALS

Card stock: white, red

Rubber stamps: 2 x 2½-inch
Christmas tree, ⅛-inch
"Have yourself a merry
little Christmas"

Dye inks: light green, dark
red

⁷⁄₁₆-inch-wide sheer light
green ribbon with white
polka dots

Paper adhesive

Adhesive foam tape

Form a 4¼ x 5½-inch card from white card stock. Cut a ½-inch slit in fold 2¼ inches from bottom. Thread ribbon through slit and tie around front of card, knotting ribbon near right-hand edge. Trim ribbon ends at an angle.

Using light green ink, stamp a Christmas tree onto a 2⅜ x 3½-inch piece of white card stock. Adhere stamped image to red card stock and trim around edges, leaving ⅛-inch borders. Adhere stamped panel to card over ribbon as shown in photo using foam tape.

Stamp "Have yourself a merry little Christmas" across bottom of card using red ink. ■

SOURCES: Rubber stamps from A Muse Artstamps and JudiKins; ribbon from May Arts.

Christmas Magic

DESIGN BY SUSAN HUBER

Form a 4¼ x 5½-inch card from red card stock.

Stamp a 1½ x 5½-inch strip of green card stock with the Christmas script rubber stamp using black ink and adhere next to the fold.

Stamp a Christmas tree onto a 1½ x 3-inch piece of white card stock using dark green ink. Adhere stamped image to green card stock and cut out, leaving a narrow border. Adhere stamped panel to card as shown using foam tape. Stamp "Christmas magic" on card below stamped panel using black ink.

Wrap ribbon around front of card, centering it over the stamped green card stock. Knot ribbon on front of card toward top and trim ends at an angle. ∎

SOURCES: Rubber stamps from Hero Arts Rubber Stamps, A Muse Artstamps and Savvy.

MATERIALS

Card stock: red textured, green, white

Christmas-themed stamps: script background, Christmas tree, "Christmas magic"

Ink: black pigment, green dye

½-inch-wide sheer red ribbon with white polka dots

Paper adhesive

Adhesive foam tape

MATERIALS

5½ x 4¼-inch white top-fold card

Card stock: light green, red

Light green/red ornaments printed paper

Rubber stamps: "Happy Hanukkah," dreidel

Ink pads: black, red

Paper adhesive

Happy Hanukkah

DESIGN BY SHERRY WRIGHT

Adhere a 5½ x 4¼-inch piece of printed paper to front of card. Referring to photo for placement throughout, adhere two 5½ x ½-inch strips of red card stock to card near top and bottom. Cut a 5½ x ⅝-inch strip of light green card stock, trimming one end slightly narrower, and adhere to card between red strips.

Stamp "Happy Hanukkah" onto red strip in lower right corner using black ink. Inside card, stamp dreidel in lower right corner using red ink. ■

SOURCE: Printed paper and rubber stamps from Paper Salon.

Holiday Cheer

DESIGN BY SUSAN HUBER

Form a 5½ x 4¼-inch top-fold card from white card stock. Tear 1 inch from bottom edge of a 5½ x 4¼-inch piece of polka-dot card stock and ink torn edge with dark green distress ink. Adhere polka-dot card stock to card front with top edges even. Stamp "holiday cheer" three times across bottom of card using dark green distress ink.

Stamp a Christmas tree on each of three 1¼-inch squares of light green card stock using black ink. Add garlands to trees using green glitter glue. Adhere each stamped tree to a 1¾-inch square of checked card stock using foam squares. Referring to photo for placement, adhere trees to card at angles. ■

SOURCES: Printed card stock from Lasting Impressions and Doodlebug Design Inc.; stamps from Hero Arts Rubber Stamps.

MATERIALS

Card stock: solid white, solid light green, green-on-green check, white-on-green polka-dot

Rubber stamps: "holiday cheer," 1 x 1⅛-inch Christmas tree

Ink: dark green distress, black pigment

Green glitter glue

Paper adhesive

Adhesive foam squares

MATERIALS

Card stock: royal blue, light
    blue

Blue-on-blue polka-dots
    printed paper

Rubber stamps: flower,
    flower outline

Ink pads: royal blue,
    turquoise

Metal "congratulations" tile

3 royal blue snaps

1¾-inch circle punch

Gem glue

Paper adhesive

Adhesive foam square

Congratulations

DESIGN BY TAMI MAYBERRY

Form a 6 x 4-inch top-fold card from light blue card stock. Adhere a 5¾ x 3¾-inch piece of printed paper to card.

Adhere a 5¾ x ⅜-inch strip of printed paper to a 5¾ x ¾-inch strip of royal blue card stock. Adhere strips to card ⅜ inch from bottom. Adhere metal tile to layered strips as shown using gem glue.

Punch three 1¾-inch circles from light blue card stock. Stamp a flower image on each using turquoise ink, then a flower outline using royal blue ink. Attach a snap through the center of each flower.

Referring to photo for placement, adhere flowers to card, attaching center flower using a foam square. ■

SOURCES: Printed paper from My Mind's Eye; rubber stamps from Stampendous; metal tile and snaps from Making Memories.

Simply for You

DESIGN BY ANDREA GRAVES, *COURTESY OF STAMPIN' UP!*

Form a 5½ x 4¼-inch top-fold card from kraft card stock. Ink edges using white ink pad.

Curl up left edge of a 5 x 1⅛-inch strip of dark pink card stock. Referring to photo for placement throughout, adhere strip to card.

Using a paper piercer or large needle, pierce holes down center of 4¼ x ⅝-inch strip of orange card stock and adhere to dark pink strip. Adhere a 4¾-inch piece of ribbon over bottom edge of orange strip and accent with staples.

Ink "for you" stamp using brown marker and stamp on lower right corner of card. Ink flowers on stamp using dark pink, orange and green markers, and stamp image onto white card stock. Trim image and adhere to label frame. Attach label frame to card using mini brads. ■

SOURCE: Rubber stamps, label frame and mini brads from Stampin' Up!

MATERIALS

Card stock: kraft, dark pink, orange, white

Rubber stamps: "for you," flowers

White ink pad

Markers for stamping: brown, green, dark pink, orange

Pewter label frame

2 pewter mini brads

¼-inch-wide yellow ribbon

Paper piercer *or* large needle

Stapler with staples

Glue

Watercolor Flower

DESIGN BY STACEY STAMITOLES

MATERIALS

Card stock: black, white, light blue

Daisy rubber stamp

Pigment inks: lavender, green, pink

⅜-inch-wide purple ribbon

Lavender picot-edge trim

Paper adhesive

Form a 4¼ x 6-inch card from black card stock and a 4 x 5-inch card from white card stock. Slide white card over black card.

Referring to photo for placement throughout, cut three pairs of notches ¼ inch apart, with 1¼ inches between pairs, through both folds to accommodate ribbons and trim. Thread ribbon and trim through holes and knot on fold.

Ink flower on stamp using lavender and green inks and stamp image onto a 2 x 4-inch piece of light blue card stock. Ink card-stock edges using lavender ink and stamp flower center using pink ink. Adhere stamped panel to card. ■

SOURCES: Rubber stamp from Hampton Art Stamps; ribbon and trim from May Arts.

Blue Dot

DESIGN BY SUSAN HUBER

Form a 4¼ x 5½-inch card from white card stock. Adhere a 4¼ x 5½-inch piece of dark blue card stock to card.

Referring to photo for placement, adhere a 2¼ x 5¼-inch piece of blue-dots-on-white printed paper and a 1¾ x 5¼-inch piece of white-dots-on-blue printed paper to card.

Stamp a flower on the blue-dots-on-white printed paper. Adhere silver-and-blue cord trim over seam between papers. ■

SOURCES: Printed papers from Die Cuts With A View; rubber stamp from Hero Arts Rubber Stamps; cord trim from Fibers By The Yard.

MATERIALS

Card stock: white, dark blue

Printed papers: dark blue
     dots on white, white dots
     on dark blue

Flower rubber stamp

Dark blue dye ink

Blue-and-silver cord trim

Paper adhesive

Adhesive dot

MATERIALS

Ivory card stock

Printed papers: yellow/white stripe, pale yellow, white-on-yellow gauze print

Daisy rubber stamp

Yellow dye ink

Yellow fiber

½-inch yellow button

Decorative-edge scissors

Needle

Paper adhesive

Adhesive dot

Simple Elegance

DESIGN BY SUSAN HUBER

Form a 4¼ x 5½-inch card from card stock. Trim ½ inch off right-hand edge of card front using decorative-edge scissors.

Adhere a 1 x 5½-inch strip of striped printed paper inside card so that it is visible behind decorative edge.

Cut a 2 x 5½-inch piece of pale yellow paper and a 1½ x 5½-inch piece of gauze printed paper. Tear off a ¼-inch-wide strip down the right-hand edge of each piece, leaving a white torn edge. Referring to photo for placement, adhere strips to left side of card front.

Wrap yellow fiber around front of card ½ inch from fold; tie ends in a bow on front.

Stamp daisy onto card-stock portion of card front using yellow ink. Thread fiber through button holes; adhere button to center of flower using an adhesive dot. ■

First Class

DESIGN BY SUSAN HUBER

Form a 5½ x 4¼-inch top-fold card from black card stock. Adhere a 5¼ x 4-inch piece of white card stock to card.

Tear along top edge of a 5¼ x 2-inch piece of script printed paper and ink torn edge. Adhere strip to white card stock, bottom edges even.

Knot black cord through hole in tag. Stamp "First Class" stamps image onto white card stock; trim around stamped image and adhere to tag. Adhere tag to card as shown using foam tape. ∎

SOURCES: Printed paper from 7gypsies; tag from Making Memories; rubber stamp from Hero Arts Rubber Stamps; distress ink from Ranger Industries Inc.; cord trim from Fibers By The Yard.

MATERIALS

Card stock: black, white

White-on-black script printed paper

2-inch-square metal-rimmed tag

"First Class" stamps rubber stamp

Black distress ink

Fine black cord trim

Paper adhesive

Adhesive foam tape

MATERIALS

Black card stock

White mulberry paper

3 x 2-inch paisley leaf foam stamp

Black distress ink

¼-inch-wide white ribbon

⁷⁄₁₆-inch-wide gray picot-edge ribbon

Die-cutting tool with ⅝-inch-square buckle die

Paper adhesive

A Wisp of Black & White

DESIGN BY SUSAN HUBER

Form a 5½ x 4¼-inch top-fold card from card stock. Stamp image onto left side of a 5½ x 3-inch piece of mulberry paper and adhere mulberry paper to card with top edge even with fold.

Die-cut buckle from card stock. Center white ribbon on top of gray ribbon and thread both through buckle. Adhere ribbons and buckle over bottom edge of mulberry paper as shown and trim ribbon ends even with edges of card. ■

SOURCES: Foam stamp from Making Memories; distress ink from Ranger Industries Inc.; die-cutting tool and die from QuicKutz.

I'd Pick You

DESIGN BY KATHLEEN PANEITZ

Adhere printed paper to card front.

Stamp framed daisies onto a 3⁵⁄₁₆ x 2⁵⁄₈-inch piece of white card stock and ink edges using black ink. Color daisies and frame using chalks. Referring to photo for placement throughout, adhere daisies panel to a 3⁷⁄₈-inch square of turquoise card stock and apply friendship sentiment rub-on transfer.

Punch two ¹⁄₁₆-inch holes through turquoise card stock and attach photo mounts with mini brads.

Adhere assembled panel to card. Tie ribbon in a 2½-inch bow; trim ends and adhere to stamped panel. ■

SOURCES: Printed paper from Bo-Bunny Press; stamp from Magenta Rubber Stamps; rub-on transfer from Lasting Impressions; ribbon from Offray.

MATERIALS

4¼ x 5½-inch ivory card

Card stock: white, textured turquoise

Yellow-and-white gingham-checked printed paper

Framed daisies rubber stamp

Black dye ink

Friendship sentiment rub-on transfer

Chalks: yellow, light blue

2 silver photo turn mounts

2 yellow mini brads

¼-inch-wide black-and-white gingham-checked ribbon

¹⁄₁₆-inch hole punch

Tiny adhesive dots

MATERIALS

4¼ x 5½-inch turquoise card

Card stock: light green, white

Purple/lavender/green circles printed paper

House rubber stamp

Light green ink pad (optional)

Colored markers

"Home is where one starts from" rub-on transfer

2⅛-inch-square silver frame

3⁄16-inch-wide green-and-white stitched ribbon

Paper adhesive

Home Is …

DESIGN BY SHERRY WRIGHT

Ink edges of a 1¼ x 5½-inch strip of printed paper and a 1⅜ x 3-inch strip of light green card stock using a light green ink pad or marker. Referring to photo for placement throughout, adhere printed paper and card-stock strip to card.

Ink house stamp with brown marker and stamp onto a 2-inch square of white card stock. Color image with markers and adhere over right edge of green strip.

Knot ribbon through hanging loop on frame and adhere frame to card, framing stamped image. Apply "Home is …" rub-on transfer to lower right corner of card. ■

SOURCES: Printed paper and stamp from Paper Salon; rub-on transfer from The C-Thru Ruler Co./Deja Views; frame from Pebbles Inc.; ribbon from Making Memories.

Just Chicken In

DESIGN BY LISA JOHNSON

Form a 4¼ x 5½-inch card from light brown card stock and ink edges using dark brown ink pad.

Fold over opposite corners of a 4 x 5¼-inch piece of red card stock. Stamp chicken tracks onto red card stock and ink edges using dark brown ink pad. Adhere to card.

Stamp a chicken and "Just chicken in" onto a 1¾ x 3-inch piece of white card stock using dark brown ink pad. Stamp seeds at chicken's feet using dark brown ink pad. Color sections of chicken using red and light brown markers and ink edges of card stock using light brown ink pad.

Tear the bottom edge off a 2 x 3¾-inch piece of light brown card stock and stamp with weathered background using dark brown ink pad. Adhere stamped chicken image ⅛ inch from top. Adhere panel to card as shown in photo.

Stamp "friend" onto dark brown card stock using white pigment ink. Heat-set ink. Punch out "friend" using word window punch, positioning "friend" at right end. Fold word window in half and attach curved ends to chicken panel with gold mini brad as shown. Flatten brad with a hammer. ■

SOURCE: Rubber stamps from Stampin' Up!

MATERIALS

Card stock: red, light brown, dark brown, white

Rubber stamps: chicken with "Just chicken in," chicken tracks, seeds, weathered background, "friend"

Ink pads: dark brown, light brown, white pigment

Stamping markers: red, light brown

Gold mini brad

Heat tool

Word window punch

Hammer

Paper adhesive

Tiny adhesive dots

MATERIALS

Card stock: green, red, kraft

Rubber stamps: flower base, flower outline, "HAPPY BIRTHDAY"

Dye inks: green, red, light brown

2 copper mini brads

¼-inch-wide sage-and-white gingham-checked ribbon

Stapler with staples

Punches: ¹⁄₁₆-inch hole, double holes, semicircular slit

Tiny adhesive dots

Adhesive foam squares

Rustic Birthday Greetings

DESIGN BY LISA JOHNSON

Form a 4¼ x 5½-inch card from green card stock.

Ink a 4¼ x 5½-inch piece of green card stock and a 4 x 5¼-inch piece of kraft card stock with green ink; ink kraft piece with light brown ink as well.

Referring to photo throughout for placement, punch semicircular slit near bottom edge of green piece; slide kraft piece into slit and adhere to green card stock.

Ink a 4 x 1-inch strip of green card stock with green ink. Punch a pair of holes near each end using double hole punch and adhere strip to kraft panel 1½ inches from top. Stamp "HAPPY BIRTHDAY" onto bottom of kraft panel using red ink; clean stamp and stamp on top of image using green ink.

Stamp two flower bases onto another piece of kraft card stock using light brown ink. Ink flower outline on stamp using red ink and stamp over both base images. Cut out, leaving narrow borders around outlines. Punch a ¹⁄₁₆-inch hole through center of each flower and attach mini brads through holes.

Crumple a 2-inch square of red card stock and ink with red ink. Ink a 1½-inch square of green card stock with green ink and adhere it to a 1⅝-inch square of kraft card stock. Staple a cut of ribbon to squares in upper left corner. Adhere squares to red crumpled square. Adhere flowers to assembled squares and adhere squares to kraft card-stock panel. Adhere completed panel to front of card. ■

SOURCE: Rubber stamps from Stampin' Up!

HAPPY BIRTHDAY

I Thought & Thought

DESIGN BY LISA JOHNSON

MATERIALS

Card stock: green, red, kraft

Rubber stamps: circle, flower outline, "I thought and thought …" sentiment

Dye inks: green, red, light brown

Antique brass mini brad

¼-inch-wide sage-and-white gingham-checked ribbon

¹⁄₁₆-inch hole punch

Tiny adhesive dots

Adhesive foam square

Form a 5½ x 4¼-inch top-fold card from green card stock. Ink edges of card and a 5¼ x 4-inch piece of red card stock with light brown ink and adhere red card stock to card.

Stamp green, light brown and dark brown circles in a curved line across the center of a 5¹⁄₁₆ x 3¾-inch piece of kraft card stock. Stamp a single circle near the bottom, 1¼ inches from left edge. Stamp flower outlines over circles in curved line using red ink. Stamp sentiment in lower right corner using red ink.

Stamp another red flower outline onto a scrap of kraft card stock and cut out, leaving a narrow border. Punch a ¹⁄₁₆-inch hole through center and attach mini brad through hole, piercing the fold in a cut of ribbon on back of flower; fold out prongs.

Ink edges and surface of stamped panel with light brown ink and adhere to card using adhesive dots in each corner. Adhere flower with ribbon over single stamped circle using a foam square. ∎

SOURCE: Rubber stamps from Stampin' Up!

Sophisticated Birthday

DESIGN BY SUSAN HUBER

Form a 5½ x 4¼-inch top-fold card from card stock. Adhere a 5½ x 1¼-inch strip of printed paper across card ½ inch from bottom of card. Apply "Happy Birthday" rub-on transfer to printed paper strip near right-hand edge.

Stamp decorative image down right-hand edge of card and ink edges of card.

Punch hole in card and attach metal flower with mini brad as shown. ■

SOURCES: Printed paper from Creative Imaginations; foam stamp and metal flower from Making Memories; rub-on transfer from Wordsworth.

MATERIALS

Green textured card stock

Green/blue/white striped printed paper

Decorative foam stamp

Green dye ink

"Happy Birthday" rub-on transfer

1½-inch metal flower

Green mini brad

Large needle *or* paper piercer

Paper adhesive

MATERIALS

Card stock: ivory, dark
yellow

Rubber stamps: diamonds
background, splatter
background, flower base,
flower center, flower
outline, "Thanks" block,
"heartfelt"

Ink pads: yellow, dark
yellow, dark purple

4 copper mini brads

Clear ultrafine glitter

¼-inch-wide dark yellow
grosgrain ribbon

¹⁄₁₆-inch hole punch

Bone folder

Tiny adhesive dots

Clear-drying glue

Heartfelt Thanks

DESIGN BY LISA JOHNSON

Form a 4¼ x 5½-inch top-fold card from ivory card stock. Stamp diamonds background on card and ink edges using yellow ink. Stamp "Thanks" in lower right corner using dark yellow ink, and "heartfelt" overlapping bottom of "Thanks" using dark purple ink. Randomly stamp splatter background using dark purple ink.

Randomly stamp flower bases onto a 5½ x 1½-inch strip of ivory card stock using yellow ink. Stamp flower outlines over yellow images using dark purple ink; stamp flower centers over stamped images using dark yellow ink. Randomly stamp splatter background using dark purple and dark yellow inks. Distress edges of stamped strip using a bone folder and curl edges using your fingers.

Punch ¹⁄₁₆-inch holes in corners of stamped strip and attach mini brads in holes. Tie ribbon around strip ¾ inch from left end and knot ends on front.

Tear the long edges of a 5½ x 2¼-inch strip of dark yellow card stock and roll edges until card-stock layers begin to separate. Ink rolled edges using yellow ink.

Adhere stamped ivory strip to dark yellow strip using adhesive dots in corners. Adhere strips to card ½ inch from fold. Apply glue over dark yellow flower centers and sprinkle with glitter; tap off excess. ∎

SOURCE: Rubber stamps from Stampin' Up!

Birthday Floral

DESIGN BY LISA JOHNSON

Form a 5½ x 4¼-inch top-fold card from white card stock. Stamp a 5 x 3¾-inch piece of white card stock with the floral background stamp using light green ink. Adhere stamped panel to a 5¼ x 4-inch piece of light green card stock.

Adhere a 3 x 2-inch piece of light green card stock to the center of the stamped panel. Tie ribbon around assembled panels and knot on left-hand side; secure with adhesive dots and trim ends at an angle. Adhere panels with ribbon to card.

Stamp label outline onto a 2¾ x 1¾-inch piece of white card stock using light green ink. Stamp "Birthday wishes" in center of frame using watermark ink; sprinkle with embossing powder and emboss. Adhere panel to card over ribbon using foam squares. ■

SOURCES: Stamps and ink pads from Stampin' Up!; watermark ink from Tsukineko Inc.

MATERIALS

Card stock: white, light green

Stamps: floral background, 2⁹⁄₁₆ x 1⁹⁄₁₆-inch label outline, "Birthday wishes"

Inks: light green, watermark

Heat tool

Silver embossing powder

⁵⁄₁₆-inch-wide light green grosgrain ribbon

Heat tool

Tiny adhesive dots

Adhesive foam squares

Cupcake Wishes

DESIGN BY LINDA BEESON

MATERIALS

Card stock: yellow, aqua

Aqua/yellow/white diamonds
    printed paper

Ink pads: black, light blue

Rubber stamps: cupcake,
    "Wish BIG"

Colored pencils

Crystal lacquer

Tag templates

Paper adhesive

Form a 4½ x 4¼-inch top-fold card from yellow card stock. Adhere a 3¾ x 3½-inch piece of printed paper to aqua card stock; cut out, leaving narrow borders. Adhere to card.

Stamp cupcake in black on white card stock; color icing and flame with yellow pencil. Coat icing and flame with lacquer. Using template, cut tag from card stock with cupcake in center. Cut slightly larger tag from aqua card stock. Adhere cupcake tag to aqua tag.

Stamp "Wish BIG" in black on white card stock. Cut small tag around words; ink edges with light blue ink.

Referring to photo for placement, adhere tags to card. ■

SOURCES: Printed paper and rubber stamps from Paper Salon; crystal lacquer from Sakura Hobby Craft; tag templates from Provo Craft/Coluzzle.

Sunflower Trio

DESIGN BY ALICE GOLDEN

Stamp three sunflowers onto a 4⅝ x 3⅞-inch piece of natural card stock using watermark ink; sprinkle with embossing powder and emboss. Adhere stamped card stock to gold metallic paper and cut out, leaving very narrow borders. Tint sunflowers with watercolor pencils and blend with watercolor brush and water.

Stamp "wishing you a very happy day" onto white card stock using light green ink. Trim around words and ink edges with gold ink. Punch hole in corner; knot ribbon through hole. Adhere tag to stamped panel.

Cut printed paper slightly smaller than front of card; adhere to card. Adhere stamped panel to card. ■

SOURCES: Printed paper from Creative Imaginations; metallic paper from Canford/Daler-Rowney; rubber stamps from DeNami Design and Hero Arts Rubber Stamps; inks from Tsukineko Inc. and Anna Griffin Inc.; ribbon from May Arts.

MATERIALS

6½ x 5-inch ivory card

Card stock: natural, white

Gold script background printed paper

Metallic gold paper

Rubber stamps: sunflower, "Wishing you a very happy day"

Ink: watermark, light green pigment, metallic gold pigment

Gold embossing powder

Watercolor pencils

³⁄₁₆-inch-wide green-and-white stitched ribbon

Watercolor brush

Heat tool

⅛-inch hole punch

Paper adhesive

Huggable

DESIGN BY JENNIFER McGUIRE

MATERIALS

6 x 4¼-inch light green card-
stock top-fold note card

Card stock: white, kraft,
yellow

Rubber stamps: flower, leaf,
"huggable," "lots of hugs"

Watermark ink

Clear embossing powder

Watercolors

½-inch flat orange button

Natural linen string

Paintbrush

Heat gun

Paper adhesive

Stamp flower and leaf onto white card stock using watermark ink. Sprinkle with clear embossing powder and emboss. Paint watercolors generously over images and wipe away extra paint; the embossing will resist the paint. Cut out flower and leaf leaving narrow borders around embossed outlines; set aside.

Stamp "huggable" repeatedly over card using watermark ink.

Cut two vertical ½-inch slits through fold in card, ½ inch apart and 1 inch from left edge of card. Push area between the slits with your fingertip so that it folds into card, creating a little "step" inside when card is opened.

Stamp "lots of hugs" onto white paper; trim and adhere to 1⅜ x ½-inch piece of kraft card stock. Adhere to top of "step" inside card.

Fold a 2¾ x 5½-inch strip of kraft card stock in half to form a 2¾-inch-square "mini card" with fold at top. Lay over fold of green card ¼ inch from left edge and adhere on front and back.

Adhere flower and leaf to a 2½-inch square of yellow card stock. Thread string through button and knot ends on front. Adhere button to center of flower. Adhere flower panel to kraft card stock on card. ■

SOURCES: Rubber stamps from Hero Arts Rubber Stamps; watermark ink from Tsukineko Inc.

Elegant Embossing

DESIGN BY ALICE GOLDEN

Stamp medallion onto black card stock using watermark ink; sprinkle with gold embossing powder and emboss. Trim, leaving ¹⁄₁₆-inch black border around edges of stamped image.

Adhere two 1⅝-inch squares of gold metallic paper to black card stock and trim, leaving very narrow borders. Adhere one of the matted pairs to gold metallic paper; trim, leaving very narrow border. Referring to photo for placement, adhere the two matted pairs together, then adhere stamped medallion on top.

Cut black card stock slightly smaller than front of card; adhere to card. Adhere a 3⅜ x 4¾-inch piece of printed paper to gold metallic paper and trim, leaving a very narrow gold border. Adhere to card. Adhere medallion panel to card as shown in photo. ■

MATERIALS

4 x 5½-inch ivory card

Black card stock

Black diamonds printed paper

Metallic gold paper

1⅞-inch medallion rubber stamp

Watermark ink

Gold embossing powder

Heat gun

Paper adhesive

SOURCES: Metallic paper from Canford/Daler-Rowney; printed paper from Family Archives; watermark ink from Tsukineko Inc.

Apple of My Eye

DESIGN BY KAREN DESMET

MATERIALS

Green card stock

Apples printed paper

Alphabet rubber stamps

Brown ink pad

Watermark ink pen

Clear embossing powder

¼-inch-wide red grosgrain
   ribbon

Heat gun

Corner rounder punch

¼-inch-wide double-sided
   tape

Form a 4-inch-square card from printed paper. Round corners using corner rounder punch. Open card and lay flat, outer surface up.

Tear a 1-inch-wide strip from card stock and adhere across card as shown in photo. Ink edges of card using brown ink.

Cut apple motif from printed paper and coat with watermark ink; sprinkle with embossing powder and emboss. Referring to photo for placement, adhere apple to card-stock strip on card. Stamp "apple of my eye" onto green card stock to right of apple using brown ink.

Cut two slits in fold to accommodate ribbon. Thread ribbon through slits; tie in a bow and trim ends.

Envelope: Create a 4¼ x 4½-inch envelope from card stock and embellish with printed paper. ∎

SOURCES: Printed paper from SEI; rubber stamps from EK Success Ltd.; watermark ink pen from Tsukineko Inc.

Pucker Up!

DESIGN BY KAREN DESMET

Form a 4-inch-square card from cherries printed paper. Round corners using corner rounder punch. Adhere a 4 x 1⅝-inch strip of dotted printed paper to card. Ink edges of card using light green ink.

Stamp a 3-inch "P" onto dotted printed paper using light green ink; cut out. Coat "P" with watermark ink; sprinkle with embossing powder and emboss. Referring to photo for placement, adhere "P" to card and "shadow" letter with the purple marker. Stamp "ucker up" onto dotted printed paper strip using light green ink.

Cut two slits in fold to accommodate ribbon. Thread ribbon through slits; tie in a bow and trim ends.

Envelope: Create a 4¼ x 4½-inch envelope from card stock. Staple along one edge. Embellish with dotted printed paper. ∎

SOURCES: Printed papers from SEI, rubber stamps from Heidi Swapp/Advantus Corp. and Provo Craft; Super Tape from Therm O Web.

MATERIALS

Yellow card stock

Printed paper: cherries, multicolored dots

Alphabet rubber stamps: 3-inch "P," 1-inch lowercase letters

Light green ink pad

Watermark ink pen

Purple chisel-tip marker

Clear embossing powder

¼-inch-wide light green grosgrain ribbon

Heat gun

Corner rounder punch

Stapler with yellow staples

¼-inch-wide double-sided tape

Amethyst Thank You

DESIGN BY LISA JOHNSON

MATERIALS

Card stock: amethyst, light
green, white

Stamps: flower, "Thanks"
block

Inks: amethyst, light green,
watermark

Silver embossing powder

Ribbon: ¼-inch-wide purple
grosgrain, ⅜-inch-wide
sheer white

½-inch-square pewter clip

Bone folder

Heat tool

Paper adhesive

Adhesive foam squares

Form a 4¼ x 5½-inch card from amethyst card stock.

Ink flower portion of flower stamp with lavender ink and stem with light green. Stamp image several times down left-hand third of card.

Ink stamp as before and stamp onto a torn 2¾ x 3½-inch piece of white card stock. Huff onto stamped image and repeat stamping twice on same piece of white card stock. Ink flower outlines with watermark ink; sprinkle with embossing powder and emboss.

Distress edges of a 3½ x 4-inch piece of light green card stock using a bone folder. Adhere stamped panel to green rectangle, then roll and crumple left-hand edge of card stock over edge of stamped panel as shown in photo.

Knot short lengths of ribbon around square clip. Slide clip over folded edge of panel and adhere panel to card.

Apply watermark ink directly to a scrap of card stock. Sprinkle with embossing powder. Heat card stock from the bottom and while still hot, impress "Thanks" block into embossing powder. Remove stamp; when cool, trim closely around word and adhere over lower right corner of stamped panel using foam squares. ∎

SOURCES: Stamps and ink pads from Stampin' Up!; watermark ink from Tsukineko Inc.

Retro Hello

DESIGN BY LISA JOHNSON

MATERIALS

Card stock: green, black

Rubber stamps: dots
 background, small dot
 circle, solid dot circle

Inks: green, black

3 pewter mini brads

Adhesive foam squares

Tiny adhesive dots

Form a 4¼ x 5½-inch top-fold card from black card stock.

Randomly stamp a 4 x 5¼-inch piece of green card stock with background and solid dotted stamps using green ink and with small dot circles using black ink. Adhere stamped panel to card using an adhesive dot in each corner.

"Hello" tag: Randomly stamp small dot circles onto a 2 x 1-inch piece of green card stock using green ink. Stamp "hello" in center using black ink. Ink edges of stamped panel with green ink.

Adhere stamped panel to a 2⅞ x 1¼-inch piece of black card stock ⅛ inch from left edge using foam squares. Attach mini brads to black card stock in a vertical row ⅛ inch to the right of the green "hello" panel.

Adhere "hello" tag to card as shown using adhesive dots. ■

SOURCE: Rubber stamps from Stampin' Up!

Big Thanks

DESIGN BY JEANNE WYNHOFF

Form a 4¼ x 5½-inch card from card stock and ink edges.

Adhere a 5-inch piece of ribbon across a 4⅛ x 5⅜-inch piece of printed paper 1⅝ inches from top. Wrap ribbon ends over edges and adhere to reverse side. Adhere printed paper to card.

Referring to photo throughout for placement, adhere a blue daisy card-stock sticker to a 2-inch square cut from color blocks card-stock sticker. Adhere center from a striped daisy to blue daisy. Ink edges of a 2⅜-inch square of light blue card stock and adhere layered stickers to card stock. Adhere card stock over ribbon using foam squares.

Ink edges of a 1⅝ x ⅜-inch strip of light blue card stock and adhere to card near bottom, ⅞ inch from fold. Punch three holes in strip and attach square brads through holes.

Stamp "thank" and "you" onto card as shown. ∎

SOURCES: Printed paper and card-stock stickers from KI Memories; stamps from Creative Imaginations; ribbon from Fibers By The Yard.

MATERIALS

- Light blue textured card stock
- Green/brown/blue striped printed paper
- Card-stock stickers: 2-inch daisies, color blocks
- Rubber stamps: "thank," "you"
- Dark brown pigment ink
- 3 dark brown square brads
- ⅜-inch-wide black/beige gingham-checked ribbon
- Paper piercer *or* large needle
- Double-sided tape
- Adhesive foam squares

Admit One

DESIGN BY SANDRA GRAHAM SMITH

MATERIALS

Card stock: ivory speckled,
  black
Green/garnet/beige striped
  printed paper
5¾ x 4⅜-inch envelope
Rubber stamps: ticket, "life
  is a daring adventure"
  quotation, baseball
  collage
Black ink pad
Red colored pencil
Black fine-tip marker
  (optional)
Decorative-edge scissors
Adhesive foam dots
Computer with font and
  printer (optional)

Form a 5½ x 4¼-inch top-fold card from ivory speckled card stock. Adhere a 3¾ x 4¼-inch piece of printed paper to right-hand side of card with top and right-hand edges even.

Stamp baseball collage three times onto ivory speckled card stock. Color laces on baseballs with red pencil. Trim one image to 2¾ inches square with glove in lower left corner. Adhere to black card stock and cut out, leaving ⅛-inch borders.

Trim glove from one of the remaining stamped images; trim baseball from the third. Adhere glove over glove on matted image and baseball over baseball on glove using foam dots. Referring to photo for placement, adhere layered stamped image in upper left corner of card.

Stamp ticket and "Life is a daring adventure" on ivory speckled card stock. Trim around quotation and adhere to black card stock; trim, leaving narrow borders. Adhere to card using foam dots.

Cut out ticket, trimming ends with decorative-edge scissors. Use computer to generate or hand-print "Dad" in tiny letters on ivory speckled card stock; trim tiny rectangles around words and adhere one to each end of ticket. Adhere ticket to upper right corner of card.

Envelope: Embellish envelope using printed paper and stamped motifs. ■

SOURCES: Printed paper from Daisy D's Paper Co.; rubber stamps from Auntie Amy Stamp Co. and Paper Inspirations.

Sunflower Mosaic

DESIGN BY ALICE GOLDEN

MATERIALS

6½ x 5-inch ivory card

Brown card stock

Printed papers: yellow tiles,
   orange, olive green

9 (1-inch) self-adhesive
   mosaic squares for
   stamping

Large sunflower rubber
   stamp

Black dye ink

Watercolor pencils

Watercolor brush

Paper adhesive

Center and stamp a large sunflower image over a 3 x 3-square block of self-adhesive squares. Tint stamped image with watercolor pencils and blend with watercolor brush and water.

Referring to photo for placement, arrange stamped tiles in vertical rows of three on three 1⅛ x 3⅜-inch strips of brown card stock. Adhere strips to a 4⁵⁄₁₆ x 3⅞-inch piece of orange printed paper. Adhere orange printed paper to olive green printed paper; trim, leaving very narrow borders.

Cover front of card with another piece of orange printed paper. Cut yellow tiles printed paper slightly smaller than front of card; adhere to card. Adhere panel with stamped mosaic tiles to card. ■

SOURCE: Printed papers, self-adhesive mosaic squares and rubber stamp from Magenta Rubber Stamps.

Card Crafting Basics

Card crafting is easy, creative and fun. Collect basic tools and supplies, learn a few simple terms and techniques, and you're ready to start. The possibilities abound!

Cutting & Tearing

Craft knife, cutting mat Must-have tools. Mat protects work surface, keeps blades from getting dull.

Measure and mark Diagrams show solid lines for cutting, dotted lines for folding.

Other cutters Guillotine and rotary-blade paper cutters, oval and circle cutters, cutters that cut unusual shapes via a gear or cam system, swivel-blade knives that cut along the channels

of plastic templates, and die-cutting machines (large or small in size and price). Markers that draw as they cut.

Punches Available in hundreds of shapes and sizes ranging from $\frac{1}{16}$ inch to over 3 inches (use for eyelets, lettering, dimensional punch art, and embellishments). Also punches for two-ring, three-ring, coil, comb and disk binding.

Scissors Long and short blades that cut

straight or a pattern. Scissors with nonstick coating are ideal for cutting adhesive sheets and tape; bo scissors are best for cutting rubber o heavy board. Consider comfort—lar holes for fingers, soft grips.

Tearing Tear paper for collage, special effects, layering on cards, scrapbook pages and more. Wet a small paintbrush; tear along the w line for a deckle edge.

Embellishments

If you are not already a pack rat, it is time to start! Embellish projects with stickers, eyelets, brads, nail heads, wire, beads, iron-on ribbon and braid, memorabilia and printed ephemera.

Embossing

Dry embossing Use a light source, stencil, card stock and stylus tool. Add color, or leave raised areas plain.

Heat embossing Use embossing powder, ink, card stock and a heat tool to create raised designs and textures.

Powders come in a wide range of colors. Fine grain is called "detail" and heavier called "ultrathick." Em bossing powders will not stick to m dye inks—use pigment inks or spec clear embossing inks for best result

Glues & Adhesives

Basics Each glue or adhesive is formulated for a particular use and specified surfaces. Read the label and carefully follow directions, especially those that involve personal safety and health.

Foam tape Adds dimension.

Glue dots, adhesive sheets and cartridge-type machines Quick grab, no drying time needed.

Glue pens Fine-line control.

Glue sticks Wide coverage.

Repositionable products Useful for stencils and temporary holding.

Measuring

...lers A metal straightedge for ...tting with a craft knife (a must-...ve tool). Match the length of the ...ler to the project (shorter rulers ...e easier to use when working on ...aller projects).
...uilter's grid ruler Use to ...easure squares and rectangles.

...ens & Markers

...oose inks (permanent, watercolor, ...etallic, etc.), **colors** (sold by sets or ...dividually), **and nibs** (fine point, ...lligraphy, etc.) **to suit the project.** ...r journals and scrapbooks, make ...re inks are permanent and fade-...istant.
...ore pens and markers flat unless ...e manufacturer instructs otherwise.

...coring & Folding

...lding Mountain folds—up, valley ...ds—down. Most patterns will have ...ferent types of dotted lines to ...note mountain or valley folds.
...ols Scoring tool and bone folder. ...gernails will scar the surface of ...e paper.

Paper & Card Stock

Card stock Heavier and stiffer than paper. A sturdy surface for cards, boxes, ornaments.
Paper Lighter weight surfaces used for drawing, stamping, collage.
Storage and organization Store paper flat and away from moisture.

Arrange by color, size or type. Keep scraps for collage projects.
Types Handmade, milled, marbled, mulberry, origami, embossed, glossy, matte, botanical inclusions, vellum, parchment, preprinted, tissue and more.

Stamping

Direct-to-paper (DTP) Use ink pad, sponge or stylus tool to apply ink instead of a rubber stamp.
Inks Available in pads and re-inker bottles. Types include dye and pigment, permanent, waterproof and fade-resistant or archival, chalk finish, fast drying, slow drying, rainbow and more. Read the labels to determine what is best for a project or surface.
Make stamps Carve rubber, erasers, carving blocks, vegetables. Heat Magic Stamp foam blocks to press against textures. Stamp found objects such as leaves and flowers, keys and coins, etc.
Stamps Sold mounted on wood, acrylic or foam, or unmounted (rubber part only), made from

vulcanized rubber, acrylic or foam.
Store stamps flat and away from light and heat.
Techniques Tap the ink onto the stamp (using the pad as the applicator) or tap the stamp onto the ink pad. Stamp with even hand pressure (no rocking) for best results. For very large stamps, apply ink with a brayer. Color the surface of a stamp with watercolor markers (several colors), huff with breath to keep the colors moist, then stamp; or lightly spray with water mist before stamping for a very different effect.
Unmounted stamps Mount temporarily on acrylic blocks with foam tape, hook-and-loop, paint-on adhesives or cling plastic.

BUYER'S GUIDE

Projects in this book were made using products provided by the manufacturers listed below. Look for the suggested products in your local craft- and art-supply stores. If unavailable, contact suppliers below. Some may be able to sell products directly to you; others may be able to refer you to retail sources.

7gypsies
(877) 749-7797
www.sevengypsies.com

A Muse Artstamps
(877) 783-4882
www.amuseartstamps.com

All My Memories
(888) 553-1998
www.allmymemories.com

Altered Pages
(405) 360-1185
www.alteredpages.com

American Crafts
(801) 226-0747
www.americancrafts.com

American Traditional Designs
(800) 488-6656
www.americantraditional.com

Anna Griffin Inc.
(888) 817-8170
www.annagriffin.com

Autumn Leaves
(800) 588-6707
www.autumnleaves.com

BasicGrey
(801) 544-1116
www.basicgrey.com

Bazzill Basics Paper
(480) 558-8557
www.bazzillbasics.com

Beacon Adhesives Inc.
(914) 699-3400
www.beaconcreates.com

Bo-Bunny Press
(801) 771-4010
www.bobunny.com

Boxer Scrapbook Productions
(888) 625-6255
www.boxerscrapbooks.com

Carolee's Creations & Co.
(435) 563-1100
www.caroleescreations.com

Chatterbox
(888) 416-6260
www.chatterboxinc.com

Clearsnap Inc.
(888) 448-4862
www.clearsnap.com

Close To My Heart
(888) 655-6552
www.closetomyheart.com

Cloud 9 Design
(866) 348-5661
www.cloud9design.biz

Colorbök
(800) 366-4660
www.colorbok.com

Crafty Secrets Publications
(888) 597-8898
www.craftysecrets.com

Creative Imaginations
(800) 942-6487
www.cigift.com

Creative Impressions
(719) 596-4860
www.creativeimpressions.com

The C-Thru Ruler Co./ Déjà Views
(800) 243-8419
www.cthruruler.com

Daisy D's Paper Co.
(888) 601-8955
www.daisydspaper.com

Daler-Rowney/Canford
(609) 655-5252
www.daler-rowney.com

Deluxe Designs
(480) 497-9005
www.deluxecuts.com

DeNami Design
(253) 437-1626
www.denamidesign.com

Design Originals
(800) 877-7820
www.d-originals.com

Designs by Reminisce
(319) 358-9777
www.designsbyreminisce.com

Die Cuts With A View
(801) 224-6766
www.diecutswithaview.com

Doodlebug Design Inc.
www.doodlebug.ws

Duncan Enterprises
(800) 438-6226
www.duncancrafts.com

DYMO Corp.
(800) 426-7827
www.dymo.com

EK Success Ltd.
(800) 524-1349
www.eksuccess.com

Ellison
(888) 598-8808
www.ellisondesign.com

Fibers By The Yard
(405) 364-8066
www.fibersbytheyard.com

Frances Meyer Inc.
www.francesmeyer.com

Go West Studios
(214) 227-0007
www.goweststudios.com

Green Sneakers Inc.
(908) 766-2181
www.greensneakers.com

Hampton Art Stamps
(800) 229-1019
www.hamptonart.com

Heidi Grace Designs Inc.
(866) 89-HEIDI
www.heidigrace.com

Heidi Swapp/Advantus Corp.
(904) 482-0092
www.heidiswapp.com

Hero Arts Rubber Stamps
(800) 822-4376
www.heroarts.com

Hirschberg Schutz & Co. Inc.
(908) 810-1111

Hot Off The Press
(888) 300-3406
www.paperwishes.com

Idea Tool Box/Advantus Corp.
(904) 482-0092
www.ideatoolbox.com

Imagination Project Inc./ Gin-X
(888) 477-6532
www.imaginationproject.com

Impression Obsession
(877) 259-0905
www.impression-obsession.com

Jesse James & Co. Inc./ Dress It Up!
(610) 435-7899
www.jessejamesbeads.com

JudiKins
(310) 515-1115
www.judikins.com

Junkitz
(732) 792-1108
www.junkitz.com

K&Company
(888) 244-2083
www.kandcompany.com

Karen Foster Design
(801) 451-9779
www.karenfosterdesign.com

KI Memories
(972) 243-5595
www.kimemories.com

Krylon/Sherwin-Williams Co.
(800) 4KRYLON
www.krylon.com

Lasting Impressions for Paper Inc.
(800) 9-EMBOSS
www.lastingimpressions.com

Li'l Davis Designs
(949) 838-0344
www.lildavisdesigns.com

Lost Coast Designs
(408) 244-2777
www.lost-coast-designs.com

Magenta Rubber Stamps
(800) 565-5254
www.magentarubberstamps.com

Magic Scraps
(904) 482-0092
www.magicscraps.com

Making Memories
(801) 294-0430
www.makingmemories.com

May Arts
www.mayarts.com

me & my BIG ideas
www.meandmybigideas.com

Mrs. Grossman's Paper Co.
(800) 429-4549
www.mrsgrossmans.com

Murdock Country Creations
(207) 225-2477
www.murdockcountrycreations.com

My Mind's Eye
(866) 989-0320
www.mymindseye.com

Offray & Son Inc.
www.offray.com

O'Scrap
(801) 225-6015
www.imaginations-inc.com

The Paper Co.
(800) 525-3196

Paperfever Inc.
www.paperfever.com

Papershapers
www.papershapers.co.uk

Paper Salon Inc.
(800) 627-2648
www.papersalon.com

Paper Source
(888) PAPER-11
www.paper-source.com

Paper Zone
(800) 929-7324
www.paperzone.com

Pebbles Inc.
(801) 235-1520
www.pebblesinc.com

Penny Black Inc.
www.pennyblackinc.com

Plaid Enterprises/All Night Media
(800) 842-4197
www.plaidonline.com

Posh Limited
(949) 542-7707
www.poshimpressions.com

Pressed Petals
(800) 748-4656
www.pressedpetals.com

Prima Marketing Inc.
(909) 627-5532
www.primamarketinginc.com

PrintWorks Collection Inc.
(800) 854-6558
www.printworkscollection.com

Provo Craft/Coluzzle
(800) 937-7686
www.provocraft.com

Queen & Co.
www.queenandco.com

QuicKutz Inc.
(801) 765-1144
www.quickutz.com

Ranger Industries Inc.
(732) 389-3535
www.rangerink.com

River City Rubber Works
(877) 735-2276
www.rivercityrubberworks.com

Royal & Langnickel Brush Mfg. Co.
(800) 247-2211
www.royalbrush.com

Rusty Pickle
(801) 746-1045
www.rustypickle.com

Sakura Hobby Craft
(310) 212-7878
www.sakuracraft.com

Sarah Heidt Photo Craft
(734) 424-2776
www.sarahheidtphotocraft.com

Sassafras Lass
(801) 269-1331
www.sassafraslass.com

Savvy Stamps
(866) 44-SAVVY
www.savvystamps.com

Scenic Route Paper Co.
(801) 225-5754
www.scenicroutepaper.com

Scrapworks Inc.
(801) 363-1010
www.scrapworks.com

SEI
(800) 333-3279
www.shopsei.com

Stamp Camp
(214) 330-0020
www.stampcamp.com

Stampendous Inc.
(714) 688-0288
www.stampendous.com

Stampin' Up!
(800) STAMP-UP
www.stampinup.com

Stamps by Judith
www.stampsbyjudith.com

Sticker Studio
(888) 244-2083
www.stickerstudio.com

Sugarloaf Products Inc.
www.sugarloafproducts.com

Sweetwater
(970) 867-4428
www.sweetwaterscrapbook.com

Therm O Web
(847) 520-5200
www.thermoweb.com

Tsukineko Inc.
(800) 769-6633
www.tsukineko.com

2 Peas In a Bucket Inc.
(888) TWO-PEAS
www.twopeasinabucket.com

Uchida of America
(800) 541-5877
www.uchida.com

We R Memory Keepers
(877) 742-5937
www.wermemorykeepers.com

Wordsworth
(719) 282-3495
www.wordsworthstamps.com

DESIGNER INDEX

Anna Griffin Inc.
My Love
Pink Christmas Tree
Special Deliveries

Mary Ayres
"Jingle All the Way"
Star-Studded Celebration
Vintage Noel

Linda Beeson
Adore
Blessings
Cupcake Wishes
It's All About You
My Dear Friend
Red Flower Celebration
Spring Fever
Sweet Treats
Thick & Thin
True Friend
Wish Big

Rebecca Cooper
Stamped With Love

Karen Desmet
Apple of My Eye
Congrats
Pucker Up!

Alice Golden
Autumn Greetings
Dreaming of Spring
Elegant Embossing
Embossed Sailboat
God Bless America
Just for You
Sunflower Mosaic
Sunflower Trio

Mrs. Grossman's
It's in the Bag
Best of the Bunch

Hot Off The Press
Filled With Love
Happy Birthday, Dad!
So Grateful

Susan Huber
Asian Influence
Autumn Leaves
Believe in Santa
Blue Dot
Christmas Joy
Christmas Lights
Christmas Magic
Easter Blossom
Easter Chick
Ebony & Ivory
First Class
Flowers Say Hello
Holiday Cheer

Polka-Dot Christmas
Sassy Card
Simple Elegance
Snowflake Dreams
Sophisticated Birthday
Symbols of Freedom
Tag Thanks
Thinking of You
A Wisp of Black & White
Weathered Stars

Lisa Johnson
Lavender Thank You
Birthday Floral
Comfort Your Heart
Delivering Love
Glitzy Holiday Greetings
Grateful
Harvest Hello
Heartfelt Thanks
I Thought & Thought
Just Chicken In
Love Grows
North Woods Greeting
Retro Hello
Rustic Birthday Greetings
Rustic Birthday Side-Fold

Tami Mayberry
Be Mine
Beaded Flower Congratulations
Butterfly Thanks
Congratulations
Daydream
Dreams
Enjoy!
Just Peeking In
Look Who's 40
Sing & Laugh
Snow Scene
Sunshine of Life
Thanks

Jennifer McGuire
Button Snowman
Huggable
Swinging Christmas

Dawn Moore
Baby Boy Congratulations
Enjoy Autumn
Fall Frolic
I Love You Forever
Spring Fever

Kathleen Paneitz
Floral Fantasy
Framed Love
I'd Pick You
Light Up the Holidays
Petals & Peeps
Sweet & Sassy
Tea Time
You're How Old?

Royal & Langnickel
Sugarplums & Snowman

Wendy Sebesta
Enjoy

Kris Smith
Autumn Splendor

Sandra Graham Smith
Admit One
Fresh as a Daisy
Typing Love Letters

Stacey Stamitoles
Friendship Lightens Every Burden
Grateful Greetings
Matchbook Thanks
Olive You
Vintage Christmas
Vintage Cupid
Watercolor Flower

Stampin' Up!
Happy Bird-day to You
Love Defined
Simply for You

Susan Stringfellow
Make a Wish
On Safari

Heather D. White
Bundle of Boy
Joy in the Journey
Touched by Friendship

Sherry Wright
Blue Velvet Thank You
Falling Snow
Graphic Thank You
Halloween Hello
Happy Hanukkah
Happy Valentine's Day
Home Is …
It's Your Day
Magic of the Season
Pet-Lover Greetings
Sunny Day Thank You
Sunshine & Seashells
Winter Wonderland

Jeanne Wynhoff
All About Autumn
Be Happy
Big Thanks
Friends Are Like Flowers
Harlequin Dreams
Heartwarming Greeting
Santa's on His Way
School Photos Folder
Smiles Are Springing Up
You Are So Sweet